MAGNETIC
NORTH

T0160152

First published in December 2017
Revised second edition September 2019
by Eyewear Publishing Ltd
Suite 333, 19-21 Crawford Street
London, W1H 1PJ
United Kingdom

Graphic design by Edwin Smet
Cover photograph by Alan Hustak
Author photograph by Kathy Keniston
Printed by Mega Printing, Istanbul, Turkey

The editor has generally followed
Canadian and/or British spelling and punctuation.

Set in Bembo 12,5 / 17 pt
ISBN 978-1-912477-96-8

WWW.EYEWEARPUBLISHING.COM

MAGNETIC
NORTH

THE UNAUTHORIZED BIOGRAPHY OF
JUSTIN TRUDEAU
CANADA'S SELFIE PM

ALAN HUSTAK

EYEWEAR PUBLISHING

**FULLY-UPDATED 2019
CANADIAN FEDERAL
ELECTION EDITION**

To Stéphane

Author, journalist and broadcaster Alan Hustak
was a television correspondent when Pierre Trudeau
was Prime Minister in the 1970s and 80s and as a reporter
for *The Gazette* for 25 years he also observed Justin
Trudeau's rise to the same office. Over the years his byline
has appeared in every major newspaper in Canada. He has
written more than a dozen books, among them *Titanic: The
Canadian Story* and biographies of former Alberta premier
Peter Lougheed, WWI Chaplain Canon Frederick Scott
and former Montreal mayor Sir William Hingston. He was
awarded the Queen Elizabeth Jubilee Medal for chronicling
the lives of deserving Canadian people and institutions.
Hustak divides his time between Montreal and
Fort Qu'Appelle, Saskatchewan.

INTRODUCTION

In 1980 Canadian journalist Richard Gwyn characterised Canada's then spellbinding 15th Prime Minister Pierre Elliott Trudeau as "a Northern Magus"– magus being the ancient Greek word for sorcerer.

Canada's 23rd Prime Minister, Justin Trudeau, like his father, Pierre, beguiled voters. Selfies, celebrity, self-confidence and his sunny ways carried him to an unexpected majority government in 2015. But, as he campaigns for a second term, the tidal wave of admiration that swept Justin Trudeau into office is receding.

Unlike his father, who warned him to remain always grounded, and to believe in reason over passion, Justin Trudeau appears to have become a "Northern Icarus," whose sunny ways have become a scorching political liability. The allure that lasted for four years has become a little stale and his efforts to find winning ways on the national stage for a second time seem a little repetitious.

The unlikely storm that threatens to swamp the Liberals was unleashed by two of his own cabinet stalwarts – his former Attorney General and Justice Minister, Jody Wilson-Raybould, and his Treasury Board President, Jane Philpott. Both resigned from cabinet in January 2019. But curiously both remained in the Liberal caucus for four months, free to undermine public confidence in the Trudeau government until they were finally expelled.

Both are seeking re-election as independents.

The controversy also ensnared Trudeau's principal secretary, Gerald Butts, who also resigned and it brought down Canada's highest ranking civil servant, the Clerk of the Privy Council, Michael Wernick. If that wasn't enough, Trudeau's parliamentary secretary, MP Celina Caesar-Chavannes resigned to sit as an independent in the House of Commons.

Ostensibly, it all began when Jody Wilson-Raybould, the first aboriginal to hold the justice porfolio, contaminated the political waters by steadfastly refusing to give a powerful Quebec based multinational corporation SNC Lavelin a break in court. The project management company, with 45,000 employees worldwide, is accused of fraud and of corruption of foreign officials in its dealings with the Libyan government when Muammar al-Qaddafi was in control. Should the firm be convicted of the charges it would be banned from doing business in Canada for ten years.

In an attempt to resolve the issue the Liberals introduced legislation in an Omnibus Bill designed to "address corporate integrity"– specifically to accomodate SNC Lavelin. The legislation would allow for a deferred prosecution which would have permitted the company, headquartered in Montreal, to pay a fine for its transgressions and come under the supervision of the court. Criminal charges would be deferred, as long as the company complied with a long list of conditions. The problem was, as Wilson-Raybould made it clear, the loophole could not be used because the legislation was flawed. The law does not apply to any corporation convicted of corrupt business practices outside of Canada.

The director of public prosecutions, Kathleen Roussel, refused to consider any compromise. She rejected an appeal from SNC to negotiate any remedial agreement. SNC challenged that decision in the courts. Then in apparent violation of the rules which prohibit the parties involved from getting together to discuss ongoing litigation, Lavelin representatives lobbied the PMO for a "just resolution".

It is clear from testimony before the commons committee and from tape recordings that key members of the Prime Minister's Office harassed, hounded and harangued Wilson-Raybould into dropping the criminal charges against the corporation.

Eleven of Trudeau's aides chose to ignore either due process or the independence of her office and attempted to persuade her at least 20 times to change her mind.

The hearings revealed that there was no clear line of authority in the Prime Minister's Office. They revealed a degree of competition between Trudeau's principle secretary, Gerald Butts, and his chief of staff, Katie Telford. When both were on the same page, the management style worked well, but when they were at odds with each other it was often hard for subordinates to know which of them spoke for a disengaged Prime Minister.

It is hard to tell whether it is a scandal, a screw up, or an attempt from within the Liberal party to sabotage the Prime Minister. It is a convoluted story involving white collar corporate crime that few voters can easily process.

For months Trudeau dismissed it as nothing more than a "conversation among colleagues." As it continued to fester, it became a "very unfortunate series of events," Trudeau then promised "to reflect, understand and do better," until he finally concluded that he could no longer work with people he could not trust.

A transcript of a conversation recorded by Wilson-Raybould makes it obvious that when the Clerk of the Privy Council, Michael Wernick spoke to her he mentioned the Prime Minister's "rising anxiety," about her refusal to use "the deferred prosecution thing". In the recording Wernick tells her:

> He (Trudeau) is quite determined, quite firm, but he wants to know why the DPA route which Parliament provided for isn't being used. And I think he is going to find a way to get one one way or another. So he is in that kind of mood. I want you to be aware of that. He does not want you to do anything outside the box of what is legal or proper, but his understanding is the DPA tool is there.

In other words, Wilson-Raybould was being asked to find a loophole to give Lavelin a break, a loophole which she made clear wasn't there. Wilson-Raybould had already stared down

Trudeau in a meeting the previous September and made it clear to him that there was no guarantee that there would be a DPA on this or any other case and that she did not feel it appropriate for her to use the tool. On the recording she is heard to say:

> This is a constitutional principle of prosecutorial independence… this conversation and previous conversations I have had with the Prime Minister and many other people around it – it is entirely inappropriate and it is political interference… what I am trying to do is protect him.

She then issues "a stern warning."

> Does he understand the gravity of what this potentially could mean? This is not about saving jobs, this is like breaching a constitutional principle or prosecutorial independence.

Wernick replies "Well I don't think he sees it like that."

"Then no one is explaining that to him Michael."

If no one explained things to Trudeau it is because no one dared. For those on Parliament Hill in the know the signs of Trudeau's dysfunctional office were there all along if anyone cared to look. Four months earlier, in September 2018, Trudeau reminded Wilson-Raybould that there was an election coming, and that if she allowed the prosecution to go ahead "there would be consequences", because "I am an MP in Quebec." The threat was implicit. She warned Trudeau then that he was interfering with her role as Attorney General and stared him down in cabinet meetings as she stongly advised him against it.

Whatever his talents as clickbait, a strong case can be made that Trudeau regards his office as ceremonial and has neglected the governing side of his job. He rid the party of its old guard, its senior advisors and senators, and put his trust in the two novices who brought him to power: Gerald Butts and his chief of staff, Katie Telford, brillliant political strategists and architects of the party's push for gender equality. Although Butts resigned from the Prime Minister's Office, he remains a key member of the Liberal Party's campaign team.

Wilson-Raybould was an unknown when Butts recruited her to run for the Liberals. Trudeau elevated her and named her Justice Minister and Attorney General. A member of the west coast Kwakiutl First Nation, Wilson-Raybould comes from a long line of tribal matriarchs. She describes herself as "a truth teller in accordance with the laws and traditions of our Big House." She was taught as a child to hold true to the tribe's core values and to act with dignity. Once a regional chief with the Assembly of First Nations, she can rival Trudeau's panache. As a young girl, she ran with the bulls in Pamplona. Matters came to a head in January when Trudeau shuffled his cabinet, and offered Wilson-Raybould the indigenous services portfolio, knowing full well that she had spent her whole life denouncing the Indian Act, which as minister she would be expected to enforce. She refused. Butts then advised Trudeau that if he allowed a minister to veto a cabinet shuffle by refusing a ministry he would soon not be able to manage cabinet. His advice was not to set a precedent. He then demoted her to Veterans Affairs. One month later she resigned. As a result, the trust that existed between Wilson-Raybould and the PMO had broken down, and Butts too resigned. As did Treasury Board President, Jane Philpott, who claimed that having lost confidence in the Prime Minister she had no choice but to abide by her "core values, ethical responsibilities and constitutional obligations."

Canada's Ethics Commisioner weighed in at the end of August, 2019 and concluded that Trudeau had indeed acted improperly, and that his actions were in violation of the Conflict of Interest Act contrary "to the constitutional principles of prosecutorial independence and the rule of law."

Like Wilson-Raybould, Justin Trudeau thrives well under pressure. He still has a fighting chance to win October's election. But the electorate has grown increasingly weary of his escapades and suspicious of his competence just as they tired of Pierre Trudeau's antics after his first term in office.

Trudeau won his election campaigning as a champion of gender equality and on a promise to improve relations with indigenous communities. His handling of the SNC Lavelin affair and the insensitive dismissal of Wilson-Raybould's concerns has tarnished the Liberal brand. It has resulted in Conservative opposition ads on television resonating with the public with the simple slogan: **Justin Trudeau, Not as Advertised.**

CHAPTER ONE

Justin Pierre James Trudeau has been regarded as something of a marvel since the day he was born. He first entered Canada's consciousness on Christmas Day, 1971, a gift to the nation as the first child in living memory to be born to a Prime Minister in office. Not since 1869, when Margaret Macdonald was born, had there been an infant in the Prime Minister's residence. His father, Pierre Elliott Trudeau, was Canada's charismatic and enigmatic 15th Prime Minister, who reshaped the country in the 1980s with his Canadian Charter of Rights and Freedoms and with his constitutional policies designed to create "a Just Society."

Utterly different from any Canadian politician who had come before, Pierre Trudeau swept into office on a tide of Trudeaumania in 1968 and served as Prime Minister for 16 years.

Many saw him as a national icon, as the saviour who would keep Quebec in confederation. Detractors complained that he behaved like Christ Almighty, and if you needed proof, the timing of Justin's birth proved it.

A second-floor guest room in the Prime Minister's residence at 24 Sussex Drive in Ottawa was turned into a nursery, with a pine crib, antique rocking chair and patchwork quilt. Trudeau's office was inundated with telegrams and phone calls from heads of state, along with more hand-knit sweaters, bonnets and booties than anyone knew what to do with.

Justin was born fourteen months after his father invoked the War Measures Act in Canada to deal with a terrorist threat in Canada's French-speaking province of Quebec. In October 1970, a handful of thugs who were self-styled Quebec Front de Liberation (FLQ) freedom fighters kidnapped the British Trade Commissioner, James "Jasper" Cross, and murdered one of their own, a Quebec cabinet minister, Pierre Laporte. Asked to what lengths he would go to apprehend the terrorists responsible, Trudeau famously declared, "Just watch me". He then imposed the draconian War Measures Act and suspended civil liberties in the country in order to thwart what he called a state of "apprehended insurrection".

If, in Stephen Clarkson's memorable phrase, Pierre Trudeau "haunts us still," then his son, Justin, is an equally beguiling chimera. Father and son were both unlikely leaders – the elder a philosopher prince, a man of fierce intellect; the younger, a telegenic pugilist. A fighter with the soul of a poet. Both share a dismissive self assurance and both define the myths that guide the Canadian psyche. Gregarious but guarded, Justin, like his father has a magnetic public persona which against all odds propelled him into office in 2015, when he rode a wave of patriotic fervour to become Prime Minister as Canada observed its 150th anniversary.

Trudeau, who turns 48 in December 2019, is still a young man. Until he assumed office his critics considered him as "not ready," – as "Trudeau lite." And during this election campaign the Conservative opposition has reinforced its claim with ads that suggest that after five year in office Trudeau by his handling of the Wilson-Raybould affair (among other things) has demonstrated that he is incompetent to govern, "Way In Over His Head."

Whatever the future, by winning the 2015 election Justin has come to represent the quintessential Canadian. As veteran political columnist Lawrence Martin commented, Trudeau brough a new vitality to the land. "Today's government is young not just by age but also in spirit and, by contrast to the venomous partisanship of its predecessor, attitude."

Although Justin's French-Canadian roots can be traced to 1659 (when his ancestor Étienne Truteau, a carpenter from La Rochelle, arrived in New France) he has the right to wear a Scottish tartan. His paternal grandmother Grace was an Elliott and a descendant of United Empire Loyalist stock. She married "Charley" Trudeau, Justin's grandfather, who made a fortune in oil. His maternal grandfather, James Sinclair, was an Aberdeen Scot, a school principal's son who came to British Columbia in 1911 at the age of two. Tall, personable and good-looking, "Jimmy" Sinclair was awarded a Rhodes Scholarship and was elected to the House of Commons as a Liberal in 1940. He enlisted in the Royal Canadian Air Force during World War II and when the war was over he became Minister of Fisheries in Prime Minister Louis St. Laurent's cabinet. Justin's mother, Margaret, was the fourth of Sinclair's five daughters and thirty years younger than Pierre Trudeau when they met on a beach in Tahiti in 1967. She was 18; he was 48. A high-spirited, immature, unstable young woman who was into drugs and rock 'n' roll, she once boasted she was "too cute for her own good, too sexy."

Margaret was ill-prepared to be the Prime Minister's wife when they married in March 1971. Justin was born nine months later. He was, according to his mother, "a cheerful, bright, manically energetic little boy." When Justin was two she taught him to sing Richie Haven's song, "Freedom." However, the family was already becoming dysfunctional when Justin was still an infant in his pram. In her autobiography, *Changing My Mind*, Margaret tells of an especially chilling incident. Having slipped away from her security detail with Justin, she was caught and forcibly returned to 24 Sussex Drive to meet with her husband's fury. "Pierre told me I had to get two things immediately and absolutely straight; that if Justin or I was ever kidnapped, there would be no deal made to get us back; and that as the Prime Minister's wife and child we were extremely vulnerable to terrorists."

Justin was still a baby when US President Richard Nixon, who had no great respect for Pierre Trudeau, avoided a direct toast to the Canadian Prime Minister at a state banquet with his prescient pronouncement that rather than raise their glasses to Pierre, they raise them instead to his son, "The future Prime Minister of Canada, Justin Trudeau."

Justin had the good looks, the wealth and the family name. Canadians watched him and his two siblings, Alexandre (incredibly, also born on Christmas day in 1973) and Michel (born in 1975) grow into adolescence. The boys were raised in the official residence at 24 Sussex Drive in Ottawa where Justin's RCMP security code name was Maple 3. Pierre expected his sons to be not only mentally but also physically fit and had tumbling mats put in the basement. Justin was five years old when Pierre began giving him boxing lessons. Later the boy learned to perfect somersaults on a trampoline on the lawn behind the mansion. As a child he told his mother he wanted to grow up to be a magician.

As a youngster he travelled the world. He was five years old when he met Fidel Castro for the first time, six when Pierre took him to Canadian Forces Station Alert in the High Arctic and arranged to have him see Santa Claus at a NORAD station. He went salmon fishing on Jupiter River on Anticosti Island with his father in the company of industrialist Pierre Desmarais, one of the richest and most influential political power brokers in Canada.

It was not exactly a typical suburban upbringing.

When he was seven he came down with chicken pox while on vacation with his family in Jamaica and was flown back to Canada in a government JetStar, This, in spite of the objections of his father, who was worried about the optics should the opposition find out that the taxpayers were footing the bill. Justin was eight years old when he was first introduced to the Queen and met Margaret Thatcher, nine when he went to Mongolia, (where Pierre made him apologize to President Yumjaagiin Tsedenbal for misbehaving at a diplomatic function). That same year he met US President Ronald Reagan, who stimulated the youngster's interest in poetry by reciting verses of 'The Shooting of Dan McGrew'. He had an audience with Pope John Paul II while he was still in elementary school. Sweden's Prime Minister Olaf Palme, gave him a hunting knife. He was ten when he went on Safari in Kenya where his father had gone to attend a conference on new and renewable sources of energy. At 11 he was in Moscow for the funeral of Leonid Brezhnev, the first time he had seen a corpse. At 12 he met German Chancellor Helmut Kohl. And these were no idle vacations. Pierre helped his sons with their homework whenever he took them out of school to accompany him on foreign trips.

Justin's childhood was shaped by summer camps on Canoe Lake in the rugged Ontario wilderness run by Taylor Statten for the children of wealthy families. According to one camp counsellor, Justin was a show off who impressed camp mates with his unusual ability to throw up at will. "He could barf on command. All the other kids thought this was great. He enjoyed being the centre of attention, even then, and went to unusual lengths to get it," recalled the counsellor. And then there was also the welcome 'wilderness' experience of the Prime Minister's retreat at Harrington Lake. He recalls playing in the driveway when Princess Diana came to use the pool. "They had a rich, focussed, disciplined upbringing. They skied and they canoed," recalls Patrick Gossage, who was the Prime Minister's press secretary.

Justin was 12 years old and with his father in Dhaka, Bangladesh, on their way to a Commonwealth conference in India, where Justin became fully aware for the first time of what lay beyond the walls of privilege. It was a fleeting incident that pricked his social conscience and left a lasting impression on him. As he tells the story in his memoir, *Common Ground*, he was in a motorcade that got stuck in traffic. As the car idled in the gridlock he caught a glimpse of a tired old man who couldn't cross the street, patiently leaning on his bicycle until the motorcade started moving again. "I remember feeling an odd pang to realize that I would never know his story – where he had come from, where he was going, and what his life was with all the events, dreams and anxieties that made him every bit as real and important as I was to myself. And it struck me suddenly that he and I were just two among billions and billions of people on this planet. Everyone of us deserved to be seen as an individual, and everyone of us had a story to tell. Of all the lasting memories I have – that one – glimpsing the narrow but deep chasm between myself, the product of a privileged position and the elderly man whose most valued possession may have been the rusting bicycle he was forced to dismount, has stuck." After that chance encounter, he writes, he never again looked at his life or his circumstances in quite the same way.

By that point his parents' marriage had started to disintegrate. Following the 1974 federal election, Margaret Trudeau began to balk against what she described as the "grotesquely formal occasions" that she was forced to endure. In September of 1974 she checked herself into the Royal Victoria Hospital in Montreal for treatment of "an emotional nature." Following the birth of their third son, Michel, in 1975 Margaret disappeared on what was described as "a freedom trip" to Europe where she spent time with a previous lover. In the spring of 1976, Maggie and Pierre separated but were still seen in public together as loving parents to their boys. They appeared to be still in love during a trip to visit Fidel Castro in Cuba. But the public façade ended on their sixth wedding anniversary when Margaret skipped her official duties and went off to Toronto and New York to party with the Rolling Stones. Whether or not you agreed with Pierre Trudeau's politics public sympathy was with the Prime Minister when his wife emerged from their limousine with a black eye, claiming that Pierre had slugged her. Canadians admired Pierre Trudeau's dignified silence in the face of his wife's increasingly erratic and often embarrassing behaviour.

Margaret was diagnosed with bipolar depression and the family suffered through the indignities of the tabloid press that portrayed her as a crazed, unfaithful wife. One writer described her as "the most seditious political wife since Catherine The Great who had managed to eclipse her husband in a ceaseless campaign of self-revelation and defiant cuckoldry."

Until they divorced in 1979, Margaret lived in three rooms in the attic of the Prime Minister's official residence, where in her own words she became "poor, mad Mrs. Rochester," referring to the hidden wife in Charlotte Bronte's *Jane Eyre*. Pierre refused to give her any money so in order to support herself she tried to break into the movies, jet-setting between London, France and New York, and having an affair with the actor Jack Nicholson along the way. While she returned to be with her sons from time to time, Justin and his brothers were in the care of two nannies, Monica Mallon and Vicky Kimberley.

After Maggie and Pierre divorced, Pierre retained custody of his sons. As a child Justin was kept largely unaware of his parents marital problems. In fact he had only a vague idea of what his father did for a living. As far as Justin was concerned his dad was "the boss of Canada.' That was that. He was therefore understandably bewildered when in 1979 Canada's boss had to vacate 24 Sussex Drive – the only home Justin had ever known. The Progressive-Conservatives, led by Joe Clark, had in that year's general election won a minority government. When Justin made a disparaging remark about his father's rival, Pierre reprimanded him. "Never attack the individual. We can be in total disagreement with someone without denigrating them." And with that he marched Justin over to Clark and introduced the boy to his new Prime Minister. "It was at that point I understood that having opinions that are different from one another does not preclude being deserving of respect as an individual," Justin wrote.

Clark's government fell within a year. In 1980 Pierre Trudeau was back in office and back at 24 Sussex Drive where the boys continued to be raised by both their parents. It was an atmosphere of privilege where they led a life apart with a degree of privacy.

Justin went to Rockcliffe Park Public School, where he first became aware that his father was something special, and that by extension, so was he. One of his classmates was the future television star Matthew Perry, whose mother worked in the Prime Ministers Office. According to Perry, he and a friend bullied Justin "out of pure jealousy," and beat him up, although Trudeau claims he doesn't remember the incident. Trudeau wasn't concerned about status. He wanted to fit in. "Justin respected his father as a role model, but I think he was a little afraid of him. Pierre was in his 70s, a single parent, and he was learning to be a father when the boys were teenagers," said Marcel Prud'homme, a long time family friend, Member of Parliament, and later a senator. "He also saw how unhappy his mother was and that had an effect on him. I think he had a love-hate relationship with Pierre. He is his mother's son, a tough Scot, more of a Sinclair and an Elliott than he is a Trudeau." He was raised well. "My earliest years were trying to keep up with Justin," says his brother Alexandre, "If he could do something, dive to the bottom of pool, or paddle a canoe, or run to the top of a hill, everyone was expected to follow him and do it."

Justin was angered and distressed by changes to the family routine when his maternal grandfather, James Sinclair, whom he adored, died in April, 1984, It was the same month that his mother married an Ottawa real estate developer, Fried Kemper. Then in June, Pierre Trudeau, frustrated at what he had not been able to achieve politically and wanting to spend more time with his sons, stepped down as Prime Minister. It wasn't until Justin appeared at the leadership convention that chose John Turner as Trudeau's replacement that he saw a detailed summary of his father's achievements in a filmed tribute and understood the impact of his father's legacy. "It was extremely emotional. Extremely educational. It was the first time I heard him say 'Just watch me,' the first time I realized there had been a referendum in Quebec." Alexandre, who was also on stage that night agrees that it was "amazing to discover just how outside the loop we were when my father was in politics. For us it was never about politics. It was about growing up."

As his retirement home, Trudeau bought the art deco Cormier house in Montreal. Designed by Ernest Cormier, a leading Canadian architect who was also responsible for the Supreme Court Building in Ottawa, the house is a landmark. It is built on an abrupt slope of Mount Royal and holds an astonishing view of the city below. Three of its floors are below the street level entrance. The public rooms were on the top floor, below that were Pierre's quarters, the study and the library. The boys were one floor below and on the lowest level, in an annex, was the swimming pool. Looking after the mansion with its custom-built furniture and marble and terrazzo floors proved to be daunting. Pierre Trudeau was totally at sea when it came to simple household chores and often relied on a neighbour, Stratton Stevens, for advice. Stevens paints a picture of a spartan, almost monastic atmosphere within the Trudeau household where the three boys were kept under constant surveillance, their recreational activities supervised and their television viewing habits not only monitored but curtailed. Pierre expected peace and solitude in his house and at home the boys were discouraged from inviting friends over and engaging in normal teenage interests. And there were rules which dictated which language could be spoken, depending upon which room you were in. (French only in the salon and the kitchen; English in the corridors and the bedrooms.)

The Trudeau boys were enrolled in the same private boys' school that their father had attended, the Jesuit-inspired College Brebeuf, where Justin opted for the 1st Secondaire curriculum, and received a rigorous classical Jesuit education. He studied Latin, took catechism lessons, enjoyed history and participated in debates. But he is remembered by those teachers willing to talk as being an average student and as a 'bit of a show off' who didn't always apply himself.

As the son of a former Prime Minister Justin could not avoid being the centre of attention. Each morning the boys were driven to school accompanied by a security guard. "It was hard to be accepted at Brebeuf at the time unless you were a pure laine, Quebecois jock," says fellow classmate Marc Miller, a Member of Parliament who has known Justin since he was eleven. "Brebeuf was filled with boys filled with a ridiculous amount of hormones who were just maturing. Justin was often teased or sometimes picked on because he was out of the ordinary."

Pierre had encouraged a healthy sibling rivalry among his sons which often contributed to a competitive three way relationship. As the eldest, Justin could be a bit imperious and overbearing. There was a streak of daredevil in him too. During one stay with his mother in Ottawa he persuaded some friends to follow him on a foolhardy treck through the city's dank water diversion tunnels in the early morning hours. At Brebeuf he engineered a break-in into an abandoned mansion. The police were called, but no charges were laid. The boys were returned to be disciplined by their teachers. Long time family friend and the late senator Jacques Hebert, once dismissed Justin's antics as an example of what he called "teenage insouciance."

In truth, in the 1980s, the Trudeau name closed as many doors in Montreal as it opened suggests Stratton Stevens. The Progressive-Conservatives under Brian Mulroney were in office when Trudeau retired to Montreal. René Lévesque, the Quebec premier, was still leading a separatist government in Quebec which had disdain for Trudeau. "Justin was always a bit of an attention seeker. He knew who he was and what was expected of him, and he knew what reaction he could provoke. He was extremely sensitive to what was going on around him, a lot like his mother. Alexandre was the idealist, stubborn like his father. Michel was genuine, high spirited and emotionally open. He was the only one who wasn't a bit cowed by his standing," says Stevens. Serge Joyal, who has known the family even before Justin was born agrees. "Justin is definitely not his father," he says. "His father was cerebral – 'reason over passion', – Justin is all over the moon. He acts intuivitely and his intuition serves him well."

Justin proved to be a good judge of character, wary of those who may have wanted to befriend him for the wrong reasons. A woman who knew him during his years at Brebeuf recalls that "other than the fact that he was a Trudeau, he wasn't all that attractive. He was a bit of a geek, tall and gangly with that mop of hair. It wasn't always easy for him to fit in. It seemed as if he carried an invisible, protective shield around with him. I felt a little sorry for him."

Justin especially disliked the formal teaching style at Brebeuf which he described as "the sage on the stage" lectures. His grades in his final year were erratic; he flunked experimental psychology and did better in his English classes than he did in French, although he proved to be a better debater in the French language. He recalls being asked as an exercise by one of his teachers to argue in favour of Quebec separation, something that was anathema to his father. He managed to do it, but his heart wasn't in it.

Justin Trudeau's interest in politics was initially piqued in 1987 during his final years at Brebeuf when Prime Minister Brian Mulroney's government attempted to resolve Canada's constitutional quarrels by appeasing Quebec nationalists with the Meech Lake Accord. It would have recognized Quebec as a distinct society, and as a trade-off, offered the other provinces increased powers. Justin read the Meech Lake Accord, familiarized himself with its details, absorbed his father's position, asked questions, and sought out conversations with others before he arrived at his own conclusions.

The spirit of Brebeuf is one of high debate where students are encouraged to stake out and defend their opinions. Like his father, Justin enjoyed examining different viewpoints; while he may have disagreed with an idea, he learned to respect the individual who advanced it.

Justin was 18 when he was booed for the first time by a public audience. He had argued in a debate that while Quebec was indeed capable of succeeding as an independent country, they were better off within the Canadian confederation. The audience of Quebec nationalists roared its disapproval. Trudeau took it in his stride. "I listen to the arguments of my separatist friends, just as I listen to my father who believes in the federal state. I have my own ideas."

His reaction to the hecklers: "Everyone has peer pressure at this age. I have never been affected by peer pressure."

CHAPTER TWO

Justin Trudeau enrolled at McGill University in 1991 with the vague idea of perhaps studying law. One of the first people he befriended on campus was Gerald Butts, a coal miner's son from Cape Breton who was working on his Master's thesis on James Joyce's *Ulysses*. Butts, a down to earth but brilliant strategist, would become a trusted friend and close advisor, eventually becoming the leading architect of Trudeau's 2015 winning election campaign. Generally regarded as the smartest guy in any room he enters, and not shy about letting you know it, the two drank beer and shot pool with each other. From the beginning of their association they were brutally honest with each other. It was Butts who played a key role in getting Justin into the university's debating society. Having been profoundly disturbed by the massacre of fourteen women at the Ecole Polytechnique in 1989, Trudeau also became active in the first student run Sexual Assault Centre in Canada, based at McGill. As a member of the debating society, young Trudeau volunteered to speak about the problem of sexual abuse of women to fraternity groups and anyone else who would listen. After years of school debates he had grown tired of talking about problems and wanted to get involved and make a positive contribution to a worthwhile cause. "He was flying under the radar when he volunteered to help, but he knew who he was and that everything he would do would come under scrutiny.

His mother was herself the victim of abusive media coverage," says the centre's founder, Mary Margaret Jones. "He is as pro-feminist as a man can be. He knows that there is a world out there that has it in for women, especially women of colour and indigenous women. Feminism is a political idea based on experience and he embodies its values."

Being Pierre Trudeau's son was an overwhelming identity to contend with. While at McGill he adopted several personas in order to hide his identity, sometimes assuming the name Justin Saint Clair (a play on his mother's maiden name) or Justin Tremblay, or simply Justin, depending on the social setting. Negotiating an identity of his own was far more complicated that anyone could sense. As he put it: "Throughout my life I have tried to focus on what I have to do to be myself and concentrate on the substance of my own ideas and who *I* am. And that has left me both grounded and able to focus, regardless of perception or attention to things external."

In the early 1990s, after the failure of the Meech Lake Accord, Brian Mulroney's government attempted to do for a second time what Pierre Trudeau's government had failed to do – come up with a Canadian constitution that would satisfy Quebec. Mulroney came up with The Charlottetown Accord, which would dilute some federal powers and at the same time recognize Quebec as a distinct society within the country. Pierre Trudeau came out of retirement to denounce that idea. Justin was at his father's side in a Chinese restaurant in a working class district of Montreal on October 1, 1999 where Pierre Trudeau delivered a pivotal address, now known as "The Maison Egg Roll" speech, which effectively demolished

Mulroney's Charlottetown Accord as an idea which would "strip naked" the federal government's authority to determine national standards in the country's best interests. In his speech, Trudeau pointed out that if Quebec were to be recognized as a distinct society, it would mean that the other provinces were less than equal, and that clauses placing limits on federal spending power would mean that the poorer provinces would not be able to finance their own programs like the richer provinces. "If you approve the accord you will have 26 asteriks to settle," he said, referring to caveats in the proposal marked 'for future discussion'. Listening to his father speak, was as Justin admitted later, a learning experience that cemented his engagement with Canadian politics. But it wasn't all about politics at this time. Justin's name surfaced in the papers as one of the gung-ho finalists in a "button your fly" speed race sponsored by Levi 501 jeans. He was photographed gamely unbuttoning his jeans and striking a provocative 'sticky finger' pose. He placed second in the contest. "They raced to see who could unbutton and pull down their pants the fastest," recalls photographer Shane Kelly. "He knew who I was since I had met him many times. He was a sweet and friendly guy. He asked me 'Please don't publish the photo. My dad will be mad if he sees it'. But the photo was too cute, and I knew my editors would be mad at me if I didn't let them print it."

Following his graduation from McGill in 1994, Justin took a year off to travel. He and three friends went backpacking through Europe and a number of West African countries – Morocco, Mauretania, Mali, Burkina Faso, and Nigeria. "We had a blast," recalls Marc Miller. "It was pretty crazy in hindsight. We didn't have that much money. Justin wasn't rich. His father was. And everyone knew Pierre was cheap. So we had cash flow problems." It was an adventure not without its harrowing moments. Justin fell ill from eating contaminated tuna, he broke his eye glasses and had to repair them with duct tape, the four of them had to push a truck through the sand dunes of the Sahara, two of his friends were mugged in Mali, and another fell from a cliff in Morocco. As they crossed the border into Mauretania, customs officials demanded a 500 franc head tax from each of them. It was Miller, who "as close to gunpoint as you can get," negotiated a discount to 50 francs with the armed border guards.

For the first time in his life, while he was in Africa, no one he encountered had a clue of who he was. "We went through Africa and no one knew him, that was extremely liberating for him," says Miller. Trudeau continued his journey, crossing Russia on the Trans Siberian Express to Bejing, during which (if he is to be believed) he read *War and Peace* on the 8,000 km trip.

"He is actually an introvert," says Miller. "Go on a trip with him and all he wants to do is read a book. There are all kinds of layers to the onion that is Justin Trudeau." He is a voracious reader, attracted to fantasy novels and science fiction, stories in which "ordinary people do extraordinary things." Books by Tolkien (*Lord of the Rings*), Ray Bradbury (*Fahrenheit 451*) and Eric Van Lustbader *(The Ninja)* were among his earliest literary influences. He can quote from memory the opening paragraphs of *The Hitchhiker's Guide To The Galaxy*.

Well versed in literature, he subscribes to the Jesuit admonition to "fear the man of a single book." To commemorate his travels he had the globe tattooed on his left shoulder.

His first serious encounter with the drug culture came in Amsterdam where he smoked hashish. The experience left him ambivalent. "I am not someone who is interested in altered states. Sometimes I guess I have gotten a buzz, other times no. I'm not really crazy about it." He has been forthright about his experiences. He admits he smoked marijuana for the first time during a trip to Jamaica. "When a joint went around the room, I usually passed it on to the next person. But sometimes I had a pull on it. It is no big deal."

Justin returned from his globetrotting with a deeper appreciation and understanding of people of different cultures and with a conviction "that if we choose to emphasie it the common ground we share can dwarf any difference." He arrived at the conclusion that Canadian identity was no longer based on ethnic, religious, historical or cultural grounds, but grew out of shared values such as openness, respect, compassion, justice, equality and opportunity. "Canadians" he has written, "represent every possible colour, culture and creed and celebrate and revel in our diversity." Back from his travels in China he returned to McGill but had still not decided on a career path. He deliberately "dodged a lot things people expected" of (him) and in the spring of 1997 moved from Montreal to British Columbia, leaving his brother Alexandre behind to care for their father. (Alexandre had joined the Royal Canadian Hussars "as a learning experience" where he shared his father's stash of Cuban cigars and rum – gifts from Fidel Castro – with his fellow recruits).

Justin went off to Whistler, a tourist town in the Coast Mountains considered to be one of the continent's top ski resorts, where his younger brother, Michel was operating a ski lift. Justin had skiied Whistler as a boy where his grandfather, James Sinclair, had a creek side cabin. While working in Whistler he taught snowboarding and found a job as a bouncer at the Rogue Wolf bar. Working as a bouncer, he said, taught him the art of diplomacy. In his memoirs he claims that being a bouncer has a practical application in politics. "Whether you are trying to assert your will in a barroom brawl or in a political confrontation, the biggest obstacle to overcome is ego. Once a disagreement begins no one wants to back down. The trick is to find a way for your opponent to save face, like leaving an agressive drunk standing out in the rain waving his fist at you in triumph while you remain inside, dry and warm, getting your job done."

He took an apartment in Vancouver's South Granville district, listed his number in the city's telephone directory and decided he wanted to become a teacher. He enrolled in the University of British Columbia where he picked up his education degree before he began teaching French and Mathematics at Winston Churchill Secondary, a school recognized for its challenging curriculum – one of only three schools in Vancouver that offered French immersion. Some teachers on the staff found his casual dress, long hair, soul patch and sandals rather unorthodox and were left with the impression that the newcomer was self-satisfied and smug, When they learned who he was, they were intimidated. But according to one of his students, "Mr. Justin was popular in class: The guys all thought he was awesome; the girls all had a crush on him." He accepted his students as they were, whatever their idiosyncrasies. Britt Frandsen, who was 13 years old and into a 'Goth phase," said Trudeau was the first teacher who wasn't freaked out by her black make-up, black hair and black clothes. "He totally saw me as a normal person. Justin was like, 'great'. you're just expressing yourself. He was the first teacher who never made my appearance in class an issue."

On Friday, November 13, as Trudeau was filling in as a substitute teacher at Pinetree Secondary School in Coquitlam, his younger brother, Michel, was killed, swept away in an avalanche while skiing Kokanee Glacier in the British Columbia interior. Michel was just 23. Justin received the news of his brother's death in a telephone call from his mother. The body was never recovered and the pervasive grief in the Trudeau family was tangible at the funeral Mass in Montreal. The Trudeau family immediately threw its support behind the Canadian Avalanche Foundation and helped raise one million dollars for a memorial chalet on a hiking trail to Kaslo Lake where Michel had spent his last night. During a visit to the Kokanee Summer festival in Creston B.C. in August 2000 to accept a donation for the chalet, he made unwanted advances towards a repoter for the local newspaper, Rose Knight. In an editorial she complained that Justin had been "blatantly disrespectful," and accused him of "inappropriately handling," her. She reprimanded him in print. "Shouldn't the son of a former Prime Minister be aware of the rights and wrongs that go along with public socializing. Didn't he learn through his vast experience in public life that groping a strange young woman isn't in the handbook of proper etiquette, regardless of who she is, what her business is, or where they are?" Trudeau apologized the next day and his apology was accepted. The incident was forgotten for 18 years until it was again reported by a reporter in an attempt to embarrass him when he was Prime Minister.

The remote alpine retreat was dedicated in July 2003. It is large enough to accomodate twenty. Michel's name is the eleventh inscribed on a plaque that lists the names of all who have died in avalanches in the park.

Directly after the accident Justin sought to reaffirm, if not reinforce, his Christian faith through a 12-week Alpha Course program, an evangelistic exercise described by its organizers as "an opportunity to explore the meaning of life." His faith, he allows, remains an important part of who he is, but even as he struggles with Roman Catholic dogma, he continues to receive communion. (Some bishops have suggested that his conscience has been badly formed, which is not a judgement of his faith, and that he should only present himself for a blessing because he "obstinately perseveres" in the promotion of abortion, in violation of Section 915 of Canon Law). His position on abortion has no doubt been influenced by his mother who told *Playgirl* magazine that she had had an abortion when she was 17 after an affair with a college football player. While Justin has said he is against abortion, he believes in a woman's right to choose and sees no incongruity between his beliefs and his religion. He believes his values are consistent with church teaching. "For someone as rational and scientific and logical and rigorous as I am, to accept the unknowable and to re-anchor myself was really, really important to me. It ended up being solace at a very difficult time." Trudeau has described himself as being "Christian with an oddly empowering, divine sense that we cannot understand. My life, like everyone else's is in God's hands. I'll defend my credo to the utmost extent."

He kept a low profile on the West Coast as best he could, but reporters caught up with him when he accompanied his father to The International Conference, a meeting in Vancouver of fourteen former world leaders. He was "more polite than put off," when the *Vancouver Sun* reporter Brenda Bouw spoke with him about a political future. "I am here because I am finally old enough to appreciate what my father does, but I have very little in the way of political aspirations," he told her. "I have spent my entire life being a regular guy and I think I am rather good at it."

CHAPTER THREE

The campus of West Point Grey Academy sprawls across 18 acres in a tony area of Vancouver known as Jericho Lands and commands a wide view of the distant city skyline and English Bay. Founded in 1996 by four rich Asian immigrants to Canada, as "a little school with a big vision," West Point Grey is considered British Columbia's best elementary school. In 1999 Headmaster Clive Austin hired Justin to teach French to the children of parents rich enough to afford the tuition. "We had just lost a French teacher and I was stuck," said Austin. "It's not often you can get a qualified French teacher on short notice in Vancouver. There were obvious benefits to the school to have Justin Trudeau as a member of our staff. I didn't care if he had three eyes coming out of his head, I offered him a contract." Students there remember Trudeau as "energetic," "slightly nerdy," "eccentric" and "goofy". One tells the story of an incident when Trudeau accepted a dare to ride a skateboard down a steep slope and wiped out. "He bailed half-way down and ate shit harder than anyone I have ever seen. His dress pants and shirt were covered in mud. We were all in stitches. What kind of a teacher would do that kind of thing?"

Although Trudeau would later be described with a degree of disdain by his critics as having been little more than a "drama teacher" at West Point Grey, he was in fact only a substitute in the drama department. Trudeau scored an above average 4.0 on *Rate My Teacher,* where the average WPGA teacher's rating is 3.84. He was becoming his own man in Vancouver, emerging out from under his father's shadow. As he tells the story in *Common Ground,* "Of all of the memories I have of my father none is more poignant than when he came to visit me in Vancouver the year before he died. It felt good to show him my classroom and share with him what I was doing with my professional life. As we were about to leave the building we heard the scurry of running feet approaching from behind. We both turned to see one of my students, almost out of breath from chasing after us. As she approached, suddenly nervous, she said 'Mr Trudeau?' I had seen this sort of scene unfold thousands of times. Everywhere I had gone with my father star-struck children and adults alike approached him to seek his autograph or shake his hand. I would always stand back smiling while my father indulged the request, and I stood back now. But this young woman didn't even glance at him. Instead she addressed me. 'Mr Trudeau. I just wanted to let you know I will be late for French class.' Now I, not Mr Pierre Elliott, was Mr Trudeau to a new generation. It was a lovely, warm moment for both of us."

The following Christmas Pierre Trudeau was diagnosed with prostate cancer. The frail old lion had increasingly become absent-minded and after Michel's death seemed to have lost the will to live. He didn't let Justin know that he was ill and refused any treatment that might prolong his life. When Justin eventually learned about the gravity of his father's situation, he was given a leave of absence from academy to go back to Montreal that autumn to join his brother Alexandre and their now-extensive "shadow" family at Pierre's bedside. It included their half-sister, Sarah, who Pierre fathered with constitutional lawyer Deborah Coyne (niece of James Coyne, the second Governor of the Bank of Canada). Pierre and Deborah Coyne became close after his divorce from Margaret.

Justin wanted a degree of privacy so he crashed with a friend, Terry DiMonte, a popular Montreal radio disc jockey. "He didn't want to run the gauntlet of reporters every time he went home," said DiMonte. "He knew the funeral was going to be huge, and he needed a space of his own to prepare. My heart broke for him. So I invited him to hole up at my place. No one would ever have thought to look for him at my house."

Di Monte was the city's most popular rock 'n' roller in the early 80s who, through a chance encounter with a member of Prime Minister Trudeau's security detail, learned that Justin and his brothers regularly tuned in to his show. The security officer was no fan of rock radio. He jokingly referred to DiMonte as a "pain in the ass," because he was forced to listen to him when the boys were in his car. One morning while on the air, as a lark, DiMonte said hello to Justin. "He was listening, and got a charge out of it," says DiMonte. Soon after, Trudeau called the station's request line and DiMonte scored movie passes for the boys. Di Monte is a disc jockey, not a journalist; Justin learned to appreciate the difference. Di Monte, only a few years older, never betrayed the confidence that the young Trudeau invested in him. Di Monte says he was attracted to the teenager's intelligence: "He was very bright, even at that age. He knew the world like the back of his hand. He had a deep passion for the country, and great respect for what his father did. I think he also appreciated the fact that when I thought he was full of shit, I told him so." Trudeau's friendship with the DJ was cemented in December 1989 when the Rolling Stones brought their Steel Wheel Tour to the Olympic Stadium. As the Prime Minister's son, Justin didn't want to run the risk of pulling rank to get tickets to the show. The tabloids would have had a field day with the story. So DiMonte got the tickets for him. After Trudeau moved to the West Coast, they kept in touch by telephone. As Pierre Trudeau was dying, Justin and Gerald Butts wrote the rough draft of Justin's fifteen-minute eulogy around Di-Monte's kitchen table. "The house was filled with people, friends arriving from hither and yon until Justin had to tell them to clear out, he had work to do." Alexandre would have preferred to keep the family's grief private but, under the circumstances, that was out of the question. As Butts and Trudeau drafted the speech, DiMonte weighed in with a suggestion that perhaps the words being used were "too cold." Butts, with a certain arrogance countered, "Words don't have a temperature."

Pierre Trudeau died on 28 September 2000. Justin delivered the nationally-televised eulogy at the state funeral for his father held at Notre Dame Basilica in Montreal.

The effect was riveting.

He had honed his skills as an actor. Whether or not it was all performance or heartfelt, Justin's oration played into the national narrative. Standing before a church packed with mourners that included Cuban President Fidel Castro, former US President Jimmy Carter, Prince Karim Aga Kahn and Leonard Cohen, it was apparent that he knew what was expected of him and had prepared well for the moment. He seemed vulnerable, much younger than 28. The eulogy covered all the bases. It was simultaneously an eloquent tribute to a Prime Minister and a poignant farewell to a father. He began with Shakespeare (*Friends, Romans, Countrymen*) and quoted Robert Frost (*I have promises to keep, and miles to go before I sleep*). Pierre Trudeau, he told the nation, "Taught us to believe in ourselves, to know ourselves and to accept responsibility for ourselves. We knew we were the luckiest kids in the world and we had done nothing to actually deserve it. Mere tolerance is not enough," he continued. "We need genuine deep respect for each other and for every human being, notwithstanding their thoughts, their beliefs, their origins. That is what my father demanded of his sons and that is what he demanded of this country. *Je t'aime, Papa.*"

Trudeau was interred in the family vault in a rural cemetery at St-Remi de Napierville, fifty kilometres south of Montreal, in the same mausoleum where Justin will one day be buried. In the weeks after the internment, police received threats that the limestone tomb would be bombed and the cemetery was put under police surveillance.

Trudeau's oration sealed his identity as a celebrity. The 'Justin Phenomenon' had begun. No longer would he be able to escape the spotlight of public scrutiny. Claude Ryan, then one of Quebec's most influential opinion makers, was especially impressed. "It occurred to me that perhaps [the speech] was the first manifestation of a dynasty," Ryan said. "At the least it led me to believe that the Trudeau family has not said its last word. We may hear a lot more from this young man."

CHAPTER FOUR

Trudeau was despondent when he went back to teach at West Point Grey. The dynamics had changed. He was now somehow different. He was about to turn twenty-nine, he had inherited a modest fortune. He was free of his father's influence but drawn to his father's roots. In fact, he wanted to go back to Montreal. While he liked Vancouver and was stimulated by his students, there were some members of the faculty who felt that Justin acted out of step and didn't respect the decorum of the institution.

Six months after his father's death he outlined his approach to teaching in a motivational speech to a teachers' convention in Markham, Ontario. The role of a teacher, he insisted, was "to create a new world of people who think differently from those in the world that we live in now." Students, he said, need to be brave and take risks, and had to be taught how to think with character. The role of a teacher, he added, was to impart courage, integrity, fairness and responsibility. He pointedly criticised school administrators in general for being too focused on curriculum and who lacked the backbone to support teachers in the classroom. He received a standing ovation. But his remarks hit too close to home and irritated a number of West Point Grey's benefactors who disapproved of what they perceived as his unorthodox approach to pedagogy. While West Point Grey's headmaster, Clive Austin, recognized that Justin "was outgoing and could sway people,"

Austin didn't subscribe to his 'buddy buddy' approach with the students. What brought matters to a head was Trudeau's proposal that the school start a student newspaper. "He was passionate about the idea," says Austin. "Under the circumstances I agreed to let him be the publisher, provided that there be no disparaging comments about members of the staff or any articles that might reflect badly on the reputation of the Academy." It was a reasonable request. But when the first edition of the paper was printed it contained an article that savaged one of the English teachers, Lynne Axworthy. The administration could not fathom why Trudeau would have allowed the paper to attack Lynne, who had once been married to Lloyd Axworthy, one of Pierre Trudeau's star cabinet ministers. Austin, who described Lynne Axworthy as one of the best teachers on campus, reprimanded Trudeau for violating their agreement. "That is clearly what I asked you *not* to do," he reminded him. In his defence Justin advanced the argument that his students had the right to 'free speech.' Austin didn't buy it.

West Point Grey released Justin from his contract. Trudeau went back as a teacher on call with the Vancouver School Board and was preparing for a class at Winston Churchill Elementary on 11 September 2001 when the World Trade towers fell in New York.

Trudeau was quick to realize that the world as he had known it changed that day. One of his students recalled "that whereas every other teacher planned their day and taught as if nothing had happened, Mr Trudeau said he was not going to teach French that morning. Instead he wanted the class to talk about the global ramifications of that event. He led an open discussion as to how we thought and felt about the whole geopolitical situation. He also reminded us not to judge Muslims based on the actions of a few individuals." As Trudeau was talking to his class a military aircraft flew above the school with an ominous roar. The students fell silent. "The fear instinct, that's what's new," he said quietly.

All commercial flights had been grounded in the wake of the attack. Gerry Butts and his wife had been in California, and rented a car in order to get back to Canada. So Justin drove down to Surrey to the Peace Arch border crossing to pick up his old friend. They talked about politics and Trudeau mulled over the idea of perhaps running for office when the time was right. After some soul searching with Butts, Justin made up his mind to go back to Montreal. He was leaving Vancouver, he explained, because he had received a "whack of public speaking engagements." When pressed about the apparent contradiction between his stated need for privacy and his decision to seek a higher profile on the lecture circuit, he snapped: "I could give a rat's ass about high profile. I won't answer personal questions."

Back in Montreal he enrolled in engineering at l'École Polytechnique de Montréal and agreed to serve as Chairman of Katimavik, a youth initiative program started in 1977 by one of his father's friends, Jacques Hébert. The program encouraged youngsters between the ages of seventeen and twenty-one to do volunteer community service work. There was certainly no shortage of things for him to do. He was one of the panellists on CBC Radio's *Canada Reads*; a 'battle of the books' series in which he argued that Wayne Johnston's epic novel *The Colony of Unrequited Dreams* set in Newfoundland was the best book published that year. Trudeau poetically defended the book as "a story of barren rock upon which nothing was expected to grow, least of all a people as tragically beautiful and noble as Newfoundlanders," showing his passion for his idea of the in-built Canadian spirit of resilience, and the Canadian landscape. (The winner that year, however, was *Next Episode*, Hubert Aquin's novel about a young separatist being held for trial in the psychiatric ward of a prison.) He continued to be hound-ed by reporters about whether he was planning a career in politics. But as Trudeau told CKAC's Claire Lamarche, "Look, I'm 30-years-old, a young guy of 30 has no reason to be in politics. It's not a huge goal for me. Politics is just one tool you can use to change the world. People who expect me to do it as a matter of course don't understand my personal values. It is not because I *can* do it that I *must* do it."

In the summer of 2003 he and Gerald Butts paddled down the Nahanni River at the invitation of the Den Cho Nation which had been lobbying Canada's Parks and Wilder-ness Society to expand the park's boundaries to protect a bigger swath of the boreal forest. Justin handled the oars, navigating Hell's Gate with relative ease. Environmentalist Ed Struzik, who was also along on the trip wrote about their last day on the river:

> To while away the time on the river Justin was chal-lenged to identify the poet who wrote, 'The fog moves in on little cat's feet.'
> "Sandburg," he says before I utter the last word.
> "'He who binds to himself a joy does the winged life

destroy, but he who kisses the joy as it flies, lives in
eternity's sun rise.'"

"William Blake," says Butts.

They continued to recite and accurately identify lines
from Frost, Tennyson, Yeats, Keats and Shelley, until the line "'Bruised dreams and broken rhythms, in
a beat up Buick, but dressed like dynamite'" stumped
them.

"Bruce Springsteen."

"God I wish my father were here. This is the kind of
thing we did on our canoe trips. Not only would my
father have identified every author, he would have fin-
ished the poem and started over from the beginning."

The Nahanni excursion prompted the newspaper headline, *IS
HE PADDLING HIS FATHER'S COURSE?* Although Butts
acknowledged to the writers of the article that Justin could be
Prime Minister if he wanted the job, Trudeau cut him short.
"Politics is a circus that I want no part of. I'm not even ready
to consider it."

He did, however, dutifully show up in Toronto for
Prime Minister Jean Chretien's farewell in 2003 where he
agreed to co-host a reception for 10,000 delegates at the Liberal
party's leadership convention. ("When your Prime Minister
asks you to do something, you do it.") It was his first public
foray as a Liberal partisan. Adopting Pierre Trudeau's defiant
gunslinger stance, Justin made a positive impression on many
of the delegates as he recalled the similar farewell tribute to his
father in 1984. His speech to the convention didn't exactly rat-
tle the rafters, but it did prove to offer some insight into what

would become his approach to politics. "People consistently underestimated [Jean Chretien]," he said. "He worked that. He knew how to play down his extraordinary abilities."

Trudeau's delivery was subdued, but his mere presence and the inevitable comparisons to his father left many delegates with a positive impression. When pressed by reporters he conceded a political career was "a distant possibility," but he made it clear that he was above all a teacher who believed in making a difference. "If I feel that can be done in politics I might end up there. But I am not making any plans about it."

Following the convention he was in Ottawa for the dedication of a new federal court building named for his father. He lent his voice to a recording of *Give Peace A Chance* to commemorate the 35th anniversary of John Lennon and Yoko Ono's Bed-Peace sit-in demonstration at the Fairmount Queen Elizabeth hotel in Montreal. Justin was one of eighty artists who took part and he wrapped his tongue around the hardest phrase – Bagism, Shagism, Dragism, Madism, Ragism, Tagism – and nailed it. Proceeds from the sale of the CD went to Amnesty International. Early in the new year he attended a fundraiser for the Canadian Avalanche Awareness Foundation in Fernie, British Columbia. That spring he was hired as a freelance radio commentator for the CKAC French-language program *l'allonge du dimanche* and as a reporter for the 2004 summer Olympic games in Athens. He made it clear he was not going to talk politics: "Everyone thinks I'm an expert in it because I have been surrounded by it all my life, but I have tried to stay away from it all of my life. I need to marry, to develop my own philosophy, my own values. Remember, my father was well into his forties before he went into politics."

CHAPTER FIVE

Justin Trudeau married Sophie Gregoire, a stylish and upbeat thirty-year-old television reporter, in a traditional Roman Catholic ceremony at the church of Ste Madeline d'Outremont on 28 May 2005. Described by friends as a "loveball," she subscribes to new age philosophies, practices Hatha Yoga and has been known to consult Ouija boards. Gregoire tosses around the word 'fate' a lot and appears to have a good deal in common with Trudeau's mother. Like Margaret Trudeau, she is something of a new age flower child, refreshingly candid about her interests and eccentricities.

Trudeau's wife is a stockbroker's daughter, an only child. Born on 24 April 1975 and raised in the Laurentian community of Ste Adele as the son that her father always wanted, she was sent to pensionnat de Sainte nom de Marie, a private girls' school in Montreal, to be educated by nuns. There she suffered her share of loneliness and confusion and developed bulimia. "I knew what was happening but couldn't stop it," she told *The Globe and Mail*'s Sarah Hampson, "I remember after a couple of years I was in my bed, suffering, suffering physically and suffering mentally, but I couldn't stop it. And sad, I was just so sad. Then one night I had a revelation not unlike something out of the *Power of Now* and *A New Earth: Awakening to Your Life's Purpose* (the bestselling books by the Oprah-endorsed spiritual leader, Eckhart Tolle). I remember going to bed that night and feeling that this disease is a disease and it is not me. I did not want to associate with it; the real me was speaking to the ego, where I said, 'Hey, intelligent, magnificent creature that you are, because you are a woman you are going to love yourself and this will be your recipe for happiness'."

She had originally befriended Trudeau's younger brother Michel, and had shown up for parties at the Trudeau home but, because of their age difference, at the time Justin did not really pay much attention to her.

She obtained a degree from McGill University, worked as a personal shopper for Holt-Renfrew, an upscale department store chain, and was hired as the Quebec correspondent for *E-talk Daily,* an entertainment show. Producer Jeffrey Feldman recalls returning with her from a shoot when she wanted him to stop the car so she might rescue "an orphan chipmunk" from the side of the road. "How did she know it was an orphan?" he asked. "It was young and crying," she replied.

Sophie and Justin found themselves sharing the stage as emcees at a 2003 Grand Prix event sponsored by Mercedes Benz. Justin had agreed to emcee the event, but was mildly stressed during the evening as he tried to tame an unruly crowd, begging them to stop talking and listen to Tony Bennett sing. Gregoire cracked a coarse, bawdy joke and he was intrigued. But it was not exactly a *coup de foudre*. If Trudeau was smitten, Sophie remained hesitant. "I don't think she ever expected she would marry him," says a long-time friend. "She can be a tease, and I don't think she was prepared to be just another

Trudeau conquest." It wasn't until a chance encounter on the street later that year that the two of them went on their first date to an Afghan restaurant. By the time they wound up at a shabby karaoke bar later that evening, Justin was swept off his feet. According to Gregoire, he told her that night that she was going to be his wife.

"We didn't end up together for no reason, we share the same values, not only social causes, but about the meaning of life itself," she recalled. "We talked about what we have to do first to be happy, but for us to be happy means that we have to make other people that we love happy." Gregoire went to Athens with him, and Trudeau formally proposed marriage in October on what would have been his father's eighty-fifth birthday, after they had driven to the family mausoleum at St-Rémi-de-Napierville to mark the anniversary. When they returned to their suite at the Hotel Le St-James in Montreal Justin bent down on one knee and asked her to marry him. When their engagement was announced, *Macleans* fawned over the young couple: "Pierre's son has got himself a fiancée, or should we say a future Mrs Prime Minister."

Gregoire walked down the aisle in an ecru dress with lace motifs that accentuated a peek-a-boo glimpse of her breasts, a creation designed to her specifications by celebrated Montreal designer Nancy Wajsman. Justin wore an unconventional beige suit. During the nuptial Mass celebrated by Father Roger Brousseau the newlyweds distributed communion to an intimate group of invited guests. A choir sang Leonard Cohen's 'Hallelujah'. Once the ceremony was over the couple drove away in Pierre Trudeau's restored Mercedes Benz 300SL roadster, decorated with yellow roses and a single red rose, Pierre Trudeau's signature boutonniere. It was the same year that the heir to the British throne quietly married Camilla Parker Bowles at Windsor Guildhall. In describing Trudeau's wedding, *Macleans* magazine remarked, "If we were to design a quintessential Canadian prince he would probably look something like Justin Trudeau."

Their first home was an unpretentious duplex on McCulloch Avenue in Outremont (a posh French-speaking part of Montreal). Gregoire was non-committal about the prospects of embarking on a political career with her husband. "It may be a path and it may not. It is too far away to put myself emotionally in that situation," she said. "But I have total faith that I will be able to handle it and adapt. Justin has integrity, honesty and amazing judgement. But sometimes I think he's just maybe too sensitive, and that is kind of scary." She said later her role was "to be there for Justin, as a partner, as a lover, as a wife to help him keep a perspective on what he does. I need to be there to remind him of our mission, of his objectives as a human being and a political man."

When they returned from a month-long honeymoon in the Seychelles, Trudeau returned to work with the Volunteer Youth Coalition and tried to drum up support for a national service policy for young people. "Anyone willing to give up a year of their life to serve their country, to make the world a better place, to learn to grow and to make a difference, should be given that opportunity," he insisted. Although Trudeau and his wife were privileged individuals, by their own admission, nothing about the marriage came easily. She expected stress, but not the degree of public scrutiny that came with being married to a public figure. She had to address carping criticism because she chose to adopt her husband's name and be known as Sophie Gregoire-Trudeau. Under Quebec's civil code it is illegal to do so. Both spouses must "exercise their respective civil rights" under the names they were given at birth.

After she was quoted as saying that she believes "a person is both male and female – the perfect balance of the two," there were rumours that both she and Justin were bisexual and in an open marriage. Trudeau laughed off the suggestion. "Gossip can't hurt people," he said. "I'd worry if there was substance to the rumours."

The most difficult hurdle, it seems, was to reconcile their different personalities and become a team. Under stress, Justin becomes reserved, self-absorbed and retreats into himself; Sophie is the opposite. When he is at work he is completely focused, and tends to ignore the needs of those around him.

Six months after Justin Trudeau was married, Paul Martin's Liberal government went down: defeated by a vote of no confidence in the House of Commons, which forced a general election in January 2006. Although the party had taken a hit in Quebec due to a spending scandal, Martin had still had a slight edge going into the campaign. However, the day before Christmas Eve the Royal Canadian Mounted Police announced that it had launched a criminal investigation into unspecified allegations made against one of Martin's most trustworthy ministers, Ralph Goodale. There is still lingering suspicion that the RCMP Commissioner, Giuliano Zaccardelli, interfered to sabotage Paul Martin's election campaign. The allegations against Goodale eventually proved to be groundless, but the mere suggestion that he was corrupt became the dominant campaign issue. The conservative leader Stephen Harper, who had put together a coalition of born-again Christians, right-wing conservatives and disenchanted Liberals, made substantial gains in the final weeks of the campaign. It was a devastating and sudden reversal of fortune for the Liberals, who had been in office for 13 years.

The day before the election, Justin Trudeau was at the Aboriginal Resource Centre in Guelph, Ontario, where he weighed in with his thoughts. While he didn't think Harper's Conservatives represented Canadian values, he recognized the Liberals were in trouble. "There is going to be a need for deep change within a lot of the structure that surrounds the Liberal party," he told the local newspaper. "People need to be entertained with new ideas and solutions."

When the ballots were counted the Liberals lost thirty seats (twenty-one in Ontario), Harper's Conservatives gained twenty-six and wound up with 124 seats, thirty-one seats short of a majority – the smallest minority government in Canadian history.

The Liberals, with their 103 seats, replaced the Conservatives as the official opposition. Martin resigned. The convention to replace him was called for December 2006. And from the moment of Martin's departure the stars that led to Justin Trudeau's political ascendency began to align. The *Guelph Mercury* was one of the first newspapers to suggest editorially that Justin Trudeau, "with his inexplicable mix of honesty, eloquence and star power" would be an ideal candidate to lead the party. "Canada needs to look to some fresh political leaders. Do Canadians a favour and come in from the political hinterland and run for political office."

But that was entirely out of the question. Sophie was pregnant with their first son. They wanted to raise a family. As proof of this, there were few public appearances that year, although in June Trudeau went to Valemount to attend the dedication of Mount Pierre Elliott Trudeau, a 2,490 metre peak named for his father in British Columbia's Premier Range of the Cariboo Mountains. Apparently avoiding politics, he spent the summer making his debut as a professional actor, having accepted an offer from the Canadian Broadcasting Corporation to portray Talbot Mercer Papineau, a dashing, pedigreed French-Canadian hero of the First World War, in a $4.3-million made-for-television series, *The Great War*. And yet this part almost seems like typecasting. Talbot Papineau was one of those great might-have-beens in Canadian history. Many believe he would have become leader of the Liberal Party in 1919 instead of Mackenzie King had he not been killed at Passchendaele. King, who went on to become the country's longest serving Prime Minister, himself acknowledged that Papineau was "the most brilliant man in Canada" and said that, had Papineau lived... King "would have been proud to have served in a cabinet with Talbot Papineau as Prime Minister."

Director Brian McKenna wanted a handsome, bilingual actor in his thirties for the role and claims he had auditioned dozens of actors but he wasn't satisfied with any of them. "Someone said, 'what about Justin Trudeau?' I laughed at first, but we called to see if he would be interested," says McKenna. "When he auditioned for us there was silence. He just stole the part."

Trudeau understood his limitations as an actor. He agreed to step into the role, he said, not only because he was "a bit of a ham" but also because he shared many of the things that Papineau stood for and believed in. "Like me he had a certain heritage around the family name, he had an English-speaking mother, and we are both talkers, with a similar energy. I understood not only Talbot's passion for life, but also his keen sense of immediate responsibility. He was torn between a cushy staff job where he could write reports or be with his men in the trenches. It was like 'I could stay with the staff appointment and come out of this unscathed, or I could do what was necessary and right.' Anytime I take on a project it is because I think that in doing so I am able to say something that will add to people's understanding of the world."

He was not unaware of the pitfalls of movie making. His mother's attempt to kick-start a film career after her divorce (in *Kings and Desperate Men*) proved to be an embarrassing experience. But unlike Margaret Trudeau, Justin was not camera shy. "I have been ignoring the cameras since I was four years old, so from a certain perspective that has helped," he told reporters who arrived on the set the first day of the shoot in mid-July. "I would be incapable of playing a role that I couldn't identify with, and that is why I was sort of safe with this one. I relate to Papineau's sense of responsibility. It is all about the importance of fighting and building a nation with it… we are talking about the founding of a country and the birth pangs of a nation. My sense of Canada as a peaceful country is tied to the fact that in order to be a peaceful country, we have a noble and glorious history in war which we are forgetting."

In make-up and uniform Trudeau resembled the real Talbot Papineau, but he himself thought he looked more like his grandfather, "Jimmy" Sinclair. During the shoot, Trudeau refused a stunt double. In one scene he slept with live rats, and in another he went skinny dipping with a number of other men. McKenna insists there was nothing gratuitous about the nudity: "It was something that really happened with Papineau during the war on a hot summer day when he told the boys to get out of uniform and go for a swim." When McKenna proposed the idea of the nude scene he expected Trudeau to refuse. "He thought about it for a moment, and said 'yes'. He said he would bare his ass if the others would. It was a terrific experience." Having done it once, however, Trudeau said later he would never do it again.

"Justin was a fine, fine actor. That's what he does, he is an actor," said McKenna. "I have worked with some of the best, and he took direction well. He knew exactly what I wanted on screen."

Shooting – and the trying-out of this particular persona – wrapped up at the end of the summer of 2006. During the promotional tour for the film, Trudeau was plagued by questions about his political future. He continued to play a cat and mouse game with the media. "I sometimes feel like running,... running away," he told *The Globe & Mail*'s Roy MacGregor.

In October, Justin again demonstrated his flair for the dramatic when he delivered the keynote address at a Public Speaking Competition at Selwyn House School in Westmount. He began by fumbling his notes and stammering. Kathleen Biggs, the teacher who organized the event and had invited him was embarrassed by his hesitant delivery. It went on for about 30 seconds, which to everyone in the room seemed like an eternity. Then Trudeau turned to Biggs with a grin and said, "Do I have you worried? I just wanted to give you an example of poor public speaking." Then he launched into a flawless delivery and gave "a rock star oration" that earned him a standing ovation. Truly, Trudeau is expert at playing the game of celebrity. His talents lie in his ability to direct focus to himself, and in his awareness of the effect he has before an audience.

In November, he was on television as the host of the Giller Awards, Canada's most prestigious literary prize, where he was introduced as our "future, uh, featured speaker" and presented that year's winner, author Vincent Lam, the $40,000 award. And, despite his denials, in spite of the years spent prevaricating, by then it was obvious that he was heading for a political career. It was now only a question of timing. "You win a lottery and you can do two things. I won the birth lottery. I got to be born to Pierre Trudeau and Margaret Sinclair.

You can either feel guilty about it and hide from it or you can say 'for some reason I was given an undue amount of power and influence that I certainly didn't ask for and didn't earn'. So then you say, 'well I have to try and be worthy of it.' I am political whether I like it or not."

CHAPTER SIX

An odd bag of contenders sought to replace Paul Martin when the Liberal leadership convention was held at the Palais des Congrès in Montreal in December 2006. The odds favoured the former socialist premier of Ontario, Bob Rae, once described as "the only candidate who can sound as if he is having a private talk with five thousand people." Also in the running was Michael Ignatieff, a tweedy high-profile academic whose father, Count Pavel Ignatiev, had been an advisor to the deposed Tsar Nicholas II in early twentieth-century Russia. Fifty-eight year old Ignatieff was born in Canada, and had been awarded The Governor General's Literary prize, but he had been living and working out of the country for twenty-five years. Convinced that Ignatieff "had the makings of a Prime Minister," Liberal party executives mounted a campaign and had persuaded him to return to Canada as a "star candidate" for the 2006 election. Then there was Stéphane Dion, an honest and decent Liberal cabinet minister who had once supported Quebec separatism, Scott Brison, an openly gay candidate who had been a Progressive-Conservative Member of Parliament, Ken Dryden, who had played hockey with the Montreal Canadiens, and two with no chance of winning: Martha Hall Findlay and Joe Volpe.

Justin Trudeau wasn't registered as a voting delegate (he hadn't yet bought his party membership) but he showed up to support a young maverick, Gerard Kennedy, who had resigned as Ontario's Minister of Education to seek the leadership. Running Kennedy's campaign was Katie Telford, the 28-year-old chief of staff, a political scientist who began honing her diplomatic instincts as a 13-year-old page in the Ontario Legislature.

Ignatieff led on the first and second ballot, with Rae in second place. On the third ballot Rae released his delegates and Kennedy threw his delegate support to Dion. And surprisingly, Dion, no one's first choice, won on the fourth ballot – collecting 2,521 votes to Ignatieff's 2,084.

Dion lacked royal jelly.

His command of the English language was limited, but as a convert to the federalist cause had he made invaluable contributions to the country as a minister in Paul Martin's government, including the Clarity Act, which makes Quebec separation from Canada almost impossible. But he lacked the stature needed to inspire confidence. The unexpected victory split the Liberal ranks even further. A number of the party's chief organizers refused to applaud his victory and stood shaking their heads at the back of the room with their arms crossed.

Katie Telford went on to work for Stéphane Dion. But she kept in touch with Gerald Butts, who by then was a policy director and principle secretary to Ontario's Liberal Premier Dalton McGinty. They became the nucleus of an informal group that began working behind the scenes to promote Justin's political strengths.

Once the convention ended, Trudeau decided he could no longer be a cheerleader, standing on the side lines waving flags and wearing Liberal party T-shirts. Subconsciously he had always been aware that he would one day run for a seat in Parliament – he was made to be at the centre of the decision-making action. Now he could no longer ignore the impulse. And besides, his career path was rather limited. He could either become a university professor or count on his personality to carry him along from one part-time job to another in the communications field.

"Now is the time for us to run," he told his old friend Desiree McGraw in early January of the new year. McGraw, an environmental policy wonk trained by Al Gore, had been actively involved in Liberal politics for more than a decade and was the chair of the Party's renewal task force on the environment. Gerald Butts was eager to help him get into the game. Many insiders suspect it was then, when Trudeau agreed to become part of the renewal task force in order to "learn the workings of The Hill" that the two began to map out the plan that would eventually allow Trudeau to take over the Liberal party. He had no way of knowing the lucky breaks that were in store for him. Having now made up his mind to run he kept the public guessing about his intentions. He cast himself in the role of a reluctant politician and continued to play with it. "I am genuinely torn," he told *The Niagara Review*. "It could be a possibility, but a lot of things would have to change in me and in the system first."

Then, while Trudeau and his wife were in Banff skiing at the celebrity sports invitational fundraiser with Robert Kennedy Jr., Jean LaPierre, Liberal Member of Parliament for the Montreal riding of Outremont, resigned. Gerald Butts, who is unusually gifted in being able to chart and understand what voters are thinking, confirmed that he had been "tasked with taking control of Trudeau's slip," and hinted that Justin was about to declare his candidacy in Outremont. But the Outremont riding Liberal Association had other ideas. It decided that Trudeau was too young, too green and inexperienced and really not much of an asset. LaPierre did Trudeau no favours either when in a radio interview he dismissed him as a lightweight upstart. "Justin inherited his mother's artistic talent but not his father's cerebral activities," he said. A number of newspaper columnists weighed in with their opinions, describing Trudeau as "intellectually shallow," "cloying" and at best "a side story, at worst an impediment." Phil Authier, writing in *The Gazette*, was sceptical of Trudeau's chances: "Those Canadians who love him see him as a messiah, a Pierre Trudeau incarnate, but some have grown weary of his 'I want to help save the world' line and his brooding about how hard it is to be rich and famous." Ultimately, there was no way Trudeau was going to get the nod in Outremont. He was seen to be too young, too inexperienced, and a bit of a political dilettante who had nothing of value to offer constituents.

Besides, Stéphane Dion had already hand-picked his own candidate for the riding: Jocelyn Coulon, a political science professor and an expert on military affairs.

One month later, in February, just as *The Great War* was about to premiere on national television, with Trudeau playing a celebrated war hero, he made his move. He resigned as director of the Canadian Avalanche Foundation and announced that he was going into politics. Ignoring the advice of those closest to him, and proving that he was serious, he ruled out seeking a 'safe Liberal seat.' To be fair, there weren't that many 'safe' Liberal seats to be had in Quebec following the 2006 election. The separatist Bloc Quebecois had walloped the Liberals in the province taking fifty-one seats; the once mighty Liberals were left with thirteen.

In what can only be described as pure synchronicity Trudeau began to lay the groundwork for his political debut. If he couldn't have Outremont, he would run in Papineau.

Papineau is a working class district, one of the smallest and most densely populated multi-cultural neighbourhoods in Canada. Almost half of its voters are of Greek, Italian, Spanish, Haitian or Arabic origin. The seat was held by Vivian Barbot, a Haitian-born Quebec separatist and a former President of The Quebec Federation of Women, who had scored a significant upset victory for the Bloc Quebecois by trouncing the Liberal incumbent, Pierre Pettigrew. Following Pettigrew's defeat, the riding had been all but promised by the Liberal Party machine to Mary Deros, a Greek-born Montreal city councillor and mother-of-three, who was also a member of the city's executive committee. Deros had a solid record as a community activist in the area. She first met Trudeau when she had her picture taken with him at the 2006 Liberal leadership convention. She admired him: "His father was a legend, I attended his father's funeral, and like everyone else thought Justin's eulogy showed that he had the stature to be a good politician. He is extremely warm, outgoing with people. That's not a put on; that is how he is. "

Deros began selling party memberships, then a second candidate, Basilo Giodano, the Calabrian-born editor of an Italian language newspaper, came forward. Trudeau had always been taught to know what his limits were and then to push them. On 22 February 2007 he was about to find out how far he could test those limits.

"Expectations for me will be so amazingly high for some people and so amazingly low for others that I can hardly do wrong. I will be somewhere in the middle, better than some people think, but I won't be my father," he said, when declaring himself in the running.

It was not going to be easy. The party wasn't going to go out of its way to support him, Sophie was pregnant, and early soundings in Papineau indicated that fifty-eight per cent of the voters in the constituency would be against him. Writing in *La Presse*, Yves Boisvert suggested that Trudeau was, perhaps, still a man in search of himself: "He is an idealistic young man wandering around in the big suit of his venerated father. He's asked to wear it. He can't take it off, but he is not too sure where to go with it."

Reine Hébert, who had been Jean Chretien's chief organizer, volunteered to work in the trenches with Trudeau. And he also gained from the support of Denise Handfield, described as "a smooth, Machiavellian" political operator who was considered to be the heart and soul of the Papineau riding. Handfield is a savvy, well-connected organizer who can telephone ten people and fill a church basement with a crowd. Their campaign strategy was clear and coherent: to downplay the Trudeau name and market Justin door-to-door as a conscientious, caring individual. Even Trudeau's brother, Alexandre, whose distaste for politics is well known, agreed to pitch in and help – his distaste of Stephen Harper was even greater than his contempt for politics. There is of course no question that Justin could count on his father's name to keep the support of the older generation of Trudeau loyalists, but he aimed his appeal to millenials, a core of younger, multilingual voters who had no linguistic hang-ups. This campaign would be about Justin, not Pierre.

Mary Deros felt squeamish about going head-to-head against Trudeau. There had been no advance warning from the Trudeau camp, no indication whatsoever that he had planned to run in her district. Still, she thought the fight was worth it in the interests of the party. "If he wanted the riding, I was going to make sure he would have to work for it. I made Justin work. He worked hard on the ground, you could feel the excitement. And the friction." Justin was lucky in this versatile, wily opponent; nevertheless, Deros became reconciled to the fact that she was fighting a losing battle when she overheard supporters who had donated to her campaign say they were going to vote for Justin. She soldiered on. "If I had pulled out of the race, it would have hurt the party. I was encouraged to continue and not drop out. I knew that at its core Papineau was Liberal. Liberals are numerous but they were disillusioned by all the infighting. You have to get out the vote. I was selling memberships, he was selling memberships. Interest in the race was high. It was good for the party." In the week leading up to the nomination the national media pundits scoffed at his chances of winning. The *Toronto Star* described him as "an interloper" who was being given the cold shoulder by liberals who "bristle at his star status." CTV's popular political talk show host Mike Duffy assured his viewers that the buzz that he was getting was that Trudeau was running third.

In an interview with the CBC on (political-affairs show) *The House* the day before the nomination meeting opened, Trudeau brushed aside the naysayers. "I bring a different set of skills to the table. [Mary Deros] has experience reaching out on a local level, Basilio understands the Italian community. I bring a broader experience as a teacher and as an activist at the national level and an energy and an enthusiasm and an openness of youth that I think is lacking a bit in politics these days," he told Petty. "To certain people's distress we have an open nomination, a genuine fight."

Anyone expecting a genuine fight on the floor would have been sorely disappointed. It wasn't even a skirmish. Justin won the nomination on the first ballot with fifty-five per cent of the vote. In the auditorium when the results were announced were Marc Lalonde, Jacques Hebert and Serge Joyal, all giants of the Liberal party in Pierre Trudeau's day, applauding the acceptance speech. Yet Liberal Party leader Stéphane Dion was conspicuous by his absence.

"What was achieved here in this process was to demonstrate that I am not just my last name," Trudeau told his supporters. "And just who am I? I am Justin Trudeau. I am a man with a dream for our riding, our province and our country. And I am a man who is able to draw us all together to achieve that dream."

The *Toronto Star*'s Chantal Hébert questioned Stéphane Dion's wisdom in having stood so clearly in the way of allowing Justin Trudeau to be a candidate in Outremont. The reality, she said, is that the Liberal Party was Pierre Trudeau's party and even though "Justin may not be God's gift to politics" it had been a grave mistake for Dion not to welcome him into the fold.

At thirty-five, Justin was fifteen years younger than his father when Pierre Trudeau joined the Liberal Party. Media pundits across the country focused on Justin's lack of political experience and dismissed him as "overblown," "untested" and "unproven." Typical of the widespread scepticism, *The Gazette* columnist Don Macpherson wrote, "Nearly seven years after his eulogy to his father, Justin Trudeau has yet to deliver a second great speech. Until he shows that he can, he will be to politics what tribute bands that dress up like 60s groups and play cover versions of old hits for nostalgic boomers are to music."

CHAPTER SEVEN

Justin Trudeau was now in an arena for another much bigger fight, preparing to take on contenders in his riding for the general election in 18 months. Anyone with money would have hedged their bets on Trudeau. One week after his nomination he appeared to be a political flyweight as he tripped and stumbled over the issue of linguistics in New Brunswick. He had gone to Saint John to speak to an elementary school teachers' convention where he said that it didn't make much sense for the province to have separate English and French language school systems. "Segregation of French and English is dividing people and affixing labels to people," he declared. Trudeau blithely ignored the fact that education is a provincial, not a federal, responsibility and also managed to overlook the fact that New Brunswick is unique in that it is the only province in the country where both languages have equal footing by virtue of an amendment to Canada's Charter of Rights and Freedoms. Language has been ingrained in the political debate since the Conquest in 1759. French-speaking Canadians fear an existential threat to their survival; many English resent the expense of having French "shoved down their throats." His remarks were especially offensive to the province's French-speaking Acadian population which had fought long and hard to win the right to be educated in the French language. Asked whether he still supported bilingualism he replied, "No. I am not for bilingualism." After a pause for dramatic effect he continued, "I am for trilingualism and quadrilingualism. This is more and more the reality of where we are heading." Picking a fight with educators angered Francophone voters while insulting the majority of Canadians who speak only one language, never mind the three or four, including Latin and Spanish, that Trudeau speaks.

Dion had to attempt to defend his candidate. "Justin has been operating in his own sphere as an independent person, but now he is a member of our team and it will take him time to adjust... Don't judge him by what he says in his first week in public life." Veteran powerbroker Denis Coderre, who was responsible for Liberal fortunes on the Island of Montreal, patronised Justin as "a rookie player, a work in progress... he is someone who has yet to learn to be loyal to his leader, loyal to his party and loyal to his constituents."

Whatever reservations Coderre and the party may have had about Trudeau they prevailed upon him to demonstrate his loyalty by campaigning for Jocelyn Coulon in the 19 September Outremont by-election, in an election that would prove to have knock-on implications for Trudeau. Coulon's poll numbers were sinking fast and the party brought in its so-called 'star candidates' to shore up his lacklustre campaign. Even though Justin had been treated poorly in Outremont he fell in line and pitched in like a well-trained foot soldier. But his effort wasn't enough. The 'safe seat' fell to Tom Mulcair, a former Liberal member of the Quebec National Assembly, who moved to the left when he entered the federal arena. It was a remarkable win for Mulcair, the first New Democrat *ever* to be elected to Parliament from the Island of Montreal. It proved to be the beginning of a seismic shift in Canadian politics. Ironically, because Trudeau lived in Outremont, Mulcair was now his Member of Parliament.

It was a painful defeat for the Liberals. The knives were out for Dion who was blamed for failing to retain a key stronghold that had been Liberal for 80 years. His leadership came under scrutiny, including his decisions with regards to Trudeau. "Not to have chosen Trudeau is perceived by many Liberals as pure vindictiveness," wrote one columnist who placed the blame for the defeat squarely on Dion and his "bad speech, bad advisors, and bad political instincts."

The week after the by-election Trudeau was in New York to have his picture taken for a feature in Oprah Winfrey's magazine about descendants of world leaders who represented a new generation of political activists. That same week he topped the results of a national poll that asked the question: Who should replace Dion as Liberal leader? Justin Trudeau had the approval of forty per cent of the respondents. The soundings astounded many veteran political observers, and sceptics were quick to dismiss the suggestion as 'a rogue poll.'

"Dumb," George Chandler wrote in the *Cobourg Daily Star*. "Does this truly show the mindset of Canadians across the country, that they would welcome the untried, untested Dauphin Trudeau as a possible ruler? There goes confederation."

By the end of September, Trudeau discreetly changed his Facebook profile so that it might accommodate an unlimited number of friends. Gone was his old profile photograph with the unkempt hair and sassy demeanour, in favour of a blue shirt and charcoal suit. He listed his occupation on the revamped social media page as a "Member of Parliament," although he had not yet been elected.

In an address to a crime prevention dinner in Kitchener, Ontario, Trudeau made it clear he was going to steer his own course: "The views you are about to hear are the views of me. They are *not* the views of the Liberal Party," he grinned as he launched into his favourite theme of investing in youth. If young people are turned off by politics, he said, it is because their views were not respected by the establishment. "It is the young people who are best suited to create a long term vision of the world," he maintained. "The older we get the more narrow our focus becomes."

Justin became a father in October when his son Xavier James was born on what would have been Pierre Trudeau's eighty-eighth birthday. But the birth of his son didn't interrupt his political agenda – the wheel was set in motion now. That same day, he was in Toronto where he appeared as a motivational speaker with Olympic swimming champion Mark Tewksbury, human rights activist retired Lt. General Senator Romeo Dallaire and the cast of a popular Canadian television series *Degrassi High*, where he encouraged 7,500 high school students to "lead the charge" for change.

"Young people get it. They're looking ahead long term and don't like what they see. Trust them. Believe in their energy and idealism. None of us is powerless. Not here in Canada. We have the ability to change the world, but only if we believe it. So let's start believing." Now a mother, Sophie was expected to balance a public profile with her image of a "mother as the nucleus of the family." Mothers, she explained, are the carriers of life, "the outer placenta." While Sophie went on at length talking about how "all the choices a mother makes as a consumer, a lover or a friend affect her childen," she also accepted that a nanny would be required to help raise her children.

New Year 2008 found the Trudeaus in Banff where Justin joined Alec Baldwin, Jason Priestley and dozens of other US celebrities on the slopes for the annual Robert Kennedy Jr. fundraiser. During a speech in Edmonton in January he said he found it "absolutely unconscionable" that parents "shortchanged" their children by not exposing them to a second or third language. "Young people who pick up other languages are better positioned to understand their world and their roles in it. That openness is what is going to transform the world into a place that is going to work a lot better than it does right now." The language issue is central to Canadian politics; realistically, no one seeking the office of Prime Minister can be unilingual. Since 1967, all Prime Ministers have been proficient to one degree or another in both French and English.

In February, at the invitation of the Centre for Israel and Jewish Affairs, Trudeau travelled to Israel with a delegation that included billionaire Stephen Bronfman, another influential family friend and heir to the Seagram's liquor fortune, who had signed on to Trudeau's team as a leading fundraiser. It was Justin's first time in Jerusalem, where he affirmed the "strong friendship that Canada has shown towards Israel for decades and will continue to do so in ongoing times." He engaged a deputy minister of the Israeli government in a detailed discussion about nuclear proliferation in Iraq and the relationships between the Shia Muslims, Christians, the Druze and the Sunni. His apparent knowledge of the Middle East impressed those on the junket; his insight was almost certainly informed by his brother, Alexandre, a documentary film producer and self-described "professional traveller" who covered the invasion of Iraq and whose film, *The Fence*, explored the plight of families in the West Bank.

Upon his return Justin ingratiated himself with Montreal's significant Irish community. He attended the annual Mass of Anticipation at St. Gabriel's Church in March and walked in the annual St. Patrick's Day Parade, which attracts hundreds of thousands of onlookers each year. He was all but upstaged in the parade by the immensely genial leader of the New Democratic Party, Jack Layton. Buoyed by his party's win in Outremont, Layton refused to be contained in the parade section reserved for politicians. As Layton stepped out of line to become a one-man band on his own, Trudeau jockeyed for position directly behind him. Trudeau was jeered by a group of hard-line separatist bystanders but he ignored their taunts. Two weeks later he shared the reviewing stand in his own constituency with Stéphane Dion at the Greek Independence Day celebrations, but Montreal Canadiens hockey player Tom Kostopoulos appeared to steal the show.

Trudeau's emerging star power in the rest of the country, however, could not be ignored. He was the centre of attention at an HIV fundraiser in Ottawa, a keynote speaker at a United Way event in Cobourg, Ontario, sported a kilt to the Daffodil Ball in Montreal, and spoke to the Canadian Mental Health Association in Owen Sound, Ontario where he ventured into his progressive views about climate change:

In the tens and thousands of years of human existence time has not been an issue. There has always been a tomorrow. But the tomorrows are vanishing. The rapidity with which we must evolve and adapt and shift and deal with innovations and new realities is such that we can no longer wait for crisis before we react. We need to learn the art of being proactive, to look down the road to the consequences of our actions today and act accordingly and responsibly. We in the western world who are most responsible for climate change are the ones who are going to be the last to suffer from its impact. If we wait until we are at that moment of suffering from the impact of climate change before acting, the whole world will have gone so far down that path that there will be nothing we will be able to do. While time is shrinking, so too is space. We have always had the luxury of lots of room on a planet that seemed to go on forever. There have always been new resources and places to develop – over the next hill, down the next valley, across the big sea – there was always room to expand and places to explore. Today, every square inch of our planet has been taken up and accounted for. What we have now is a closed system, and within a closed system every single action has an impact on everything else. Within this reality of shrinking space and time it is not just governments and corporations that are the cause of the problem. It's millions upon millions of small individual actions taken by people who are just trying to get by and care for themselves, people who are trying to make a better life for their loved ones, who are not aware of the greater implications of every single one of those actions. Nor is it appropriate to assign to government and corporations the sole responsibility for discovering solutions. No political leader, no matter how popular or powerful, is going to be able to change the world unless every individual is able to step up and step forward. But here is the conundrum: we live in a world where the individual is made to feel more and more powerless. In a world where the scope and scale of our problems are so vast, the individual feels overwhelmed and very small indeed. It is important for us to break out of that mindset and understand what it is to lean on each other, to build strong communities and connect, and look for the values that unite us, the common ground we all share. We need to believe in something bigger and bolder and better. We have to reach out and demand more from our leaders, but mostly we have to demand more of our neighbours and ourselves. We are fashioning our children's future now. Let's get it right.

The ideas he enunciated were almost certainly shaped by Gerald Butts, who guided Ontario Premier Dalton McGinty's environmental policies, and who served as President of the World Wildlife Fund of Canada after McGinty's defeat. Those suspicious of Butts see him as feeding Trudeau these words – but this speech has become one of the touchstones of Trudeau's administration.

For all this, Trudeau didn't expect to hit the official campaign trail as soon as he did. The Harper government had amended the Elections Act in 2007 to establish a fixed date for general elections every four years on the third Monday of October beginning in 2009. Harper maintained that fixed election dates were necessary to prevent Prime Ministers from calling snap elections (as Jean Chretien had so successfully done in 2000). However, Harper's minority was threatened with defeat, so rather than wait for the opposition to bring him down he circumvented his own rules, exercised his executive prerogative and called the election for 14 October 2008. He needed a majority, he said, to deal with the fallout of the turmoil caused in the US economy by soaring oil prices and the collapse of the housing market.

ALAN HUSTAK

The Liberals were ill-prepared for the campaign, but Trudeau went scrapping for a fight in Papineau. He brought gay activist Louis-Alexandre Lanthier on board as his wingman to run his campaign. "I don't want to be handed anything," he said. "I don't need to be handed anything. I don't expect to be handed anything. I am more than capable of bringing the fight, and it will be a chance for me to demonstrate my own political activities." When he launched his campaign on 24 September 2008, a radical separatist group, The Young Quebec Patriots, disrupted his meeting and he faced taunts from the crowds who chanted "Just In – Just Out," and "No Trudeau in Papineau."

It was by no means certain he'd win. His main rival, the incumbent Bloc Quebecois MP Vivian Barbot, was prepared for the fight. But she found Trudeau plastic: "I never encountered the real person, his tie is straight, his hair is well groomed, he has a winning smile, but beyond that he reveals nothing of himself. In any event, he only gives you half a handshake with his fingertips, it is really unpleasant." But how evidential is a mismatched handshake? Others suggest that in person, on the campaign trail, he demonstrates the personality of a cardboard cut out. He loves to be seen, to be photographed, but don't expect to engage him in a conversation.

The Liberal leader Stéphane Dion was no asset; there would be no coat-tails to ride in this campaign. Dion looked like someone afraid of his own shadow – caught on camera using a knife and fork to eat a hot dog – one gets the picture. To the public, Dion appeared insecure and unable to communicate in English, and when he spoke French came off as too much of an egghead. His so-called 'Green Shift' campaign focused on the need for an environmental carbon tax to combat global warming. Not only was it a hard sell, it proved to be a disaster. Conservative attack ads were vicious. One especially tasteless television spot featured a 'poopin puffin' defecating on 'Professor' Dion's head. Although the Conservatives withdrew the ad, the impression lingered. During the campaign, Mike Duffy, the Ottawa editor of CTV News channel, aired the outtakes of an English language interview with Dion that had been conducted earlier in Halifax. The footage revealed the exhausted Liberal leader to be confused, incoherent and apparently painfully constipated. They were, however, outtakes, false starts from a pre-taped interview, never meant to be seen. Duffy, however, thought otherwise, and once the outtakes were televised the ridicule was merciless. It proved to be politically fatal. For his role in helping Harper's campaign Duffy would be rewarded with a Senate seat.

When the ballots were counted the Conservatives had 143 seats, and the Liberals, with twenty-six per cent of the vote, took seventy-seven. Stephen Harper had won a second mandate twelve seats short of a majority. The New Democrats increased its numbers by eight seats, winning thirty-seven. The Bloc took forty-nine seats in Quebec. But this made no difference in Papineau. Justin had defeated Barbot by 1,200 votes.

He was sworn in as an MP for the first session of the fortieth Parliament, which opened in November. As all rookies he was assigned a seat in the back row of the opposition benches in the House of Commons. "This is my place right now. This is my place," he told a reporter who covered his arrival in his dingy office in the Confederation Block on Parliament Hill. "I've been working hard for this for the past couple of years. I know how hard I have worked and how much I built with the people in my riding that I am here for."

It was generally assumed that the minority parliament would be allowed to get on with its work for at least two years, enough time to allow Trudeau to learn the ropes as an MP. As he had once confided to a friend, it would take him a while to familiarize himself with "the ins and outs of the party, make my way through the snakes, and while I am doing that, begin to build a national network."

But luck and fate thought otherwise. Before the election Dion and Layton had concocted a secret deal to combine forces and immediately bring down the minority government with a non-confidence motion. Rather than force another election, the scheme they had in mind was to ask the Governor General to dismiss Harper as Prime Minister and invite Dion to replace him as head of a Liberal-NDP coalition. Under the six-point accord that had been hammered out, Jack Layton and the NDP would hold a quarter of the cabinet positions in Dion's government. Constitutionally it was doable; politically it was reckless – too clever by half. To work it needed the support of the Quebec Sovereignists. But the inclusion of Bloc Quebecois leader Gilles Duceppe proved to be the kiss of death. Any power play which required the support of Quebec separatists to succeed would appear like a desperate attempt to usurp power only six weeks after Canadians had made their choices in the polls.

Harper turned on the opposition and accused both men of "making a deal with the devil" to betray the best interests of the country. A coalition government under the threat of a veto from "socialists and separatists," Harper claimed, would hold the country up to ransom and provoke an economic crisis. Even Liberal Michael Ignatieff, who had not been party to the talks, described it as "a coalition of losers." In order to avoid facing a confidence vote scheduled for 8 December, Harper persuaded the Governor General, Michelle Jean, to prorogue Parliament until 26 January.

The attempted coup failed. Dion's own caucus rejected the hair-brained scheme and forced him out. Michael Ignatieff took over as interim Liberal Leader of the Opposition.

The following week Prime Minister Harper named eighteen senators, among them Mike Duffy, Patrick Brazeau and Pamela Wallin. It was apparently the downfall of the Liberal Party, but the key players in the forthcoming political melodrama that would see Justin Trudeau emerge in the starring role were all assembling in the wings.

CHAPTER EIGHT

Substance was not the first thing that came to mind when Justin Trudeau arrived for the second session of the 40th Parliament in February 2009, one week after his daughter, Ella-Grace Margaret, was born. He was certainly taking his political work seriously, and was not about to disappear into the backbenches, where he had little chance of asking attention-grabbing questions or being heard during question period. He always showed up for votes, and if anyone had bothered to pay attention, more often than not they would have seen his votes were consistent, often supporting Harper's legislation. However, in caucus meetings he was remembered as a "smug, smilingly silent presence" with little to offer. He seemed to spend more time outside the House of Commons grabbing headlines away from Parliament Hill than he did on it. He was bored by the daily grind of parliamentary procedures, and he continued to work the social circuit, getting noticed in the society pages as President of Maskarade, an AIDS fundraiser in Montreal, which recreated Truman Capote's black and white masquerade ball. He hit the road travelling from high school to high school, service club to service club, speaking at barbeques, dinners and receptions. Unlike his father, whose charisma was cold, enigmatic and cerebral, Justin is just the opposite. "He is like a chameleon. He fits into whatever the surroundings. He is equally at home with a blue collar or a blue ribbon crowd," observed long-time party stalwart Marcel Prud'homme, who held Trudeau's Papineau riding as an MP for 33 years. "His father was not comfortable with crowds. He was shy and not especially good at small talk or at kissing babies. Justin enjoys engaging with people, he enjoys being the centre of attention. Pierre didn't."

There was an element of narcissism in his approach to politics, but he is genuinely embarrassed by flattery. He is, however, by no means humble and has an intuitive sense that detects those who want to use him as well as those who he could use then discard to further his own aims. His direct contact with other people fuelled the energy Justin Trudeau needed to carry him along. He was creating a mythology of self, one that allowed him to slip into whatever role might be required of him for a specific occasion. He grew a soul patch for a charity drive called Movember to raise awareness for men's health issues and resembled an urban Captain Jack Sparrow. He appeared at social functions as a kilted Braveheart and wasn't afraid to bare his chest like Tarzan when he felt like it. As he became more adept in his various guises, he discovered he could usually get away with whatever role he chose to play.

By the time Michael Ignatieff was confirmed without fanfare as leader of the Liberal Party in April 2009, internal polling continued to show that Trudeau was now more popular than Ignatieff. Trudeau was ambivalent about his new leader. He recognized Ignatieff as a great intellect but was not convinced he had the necessary moxie to lead the party. Ignatieff lectured rather than listened. And his double-edged approach to human rights, as well as his support for the US government's policy of the compulsory promotion of democracy in the Middle East, was at odds with the views of the Liberal caucus. Trudeau agreed, however, to be part of Ignatieff's shadow cabinet as opposition critic for Citizenship and Immigration, but he was still eager to be seen primarily as the national spokesman on youth issues. His first legislative initiative called for a parliamentary committee to look into establishing a national voluntary service policy for young people, which would stimulate the Katimavik program. He kept repeating the same mantra: "If the youth really begin to understand their own power to act, to think, then changing the world not only seems possible, it seems inevitable."

Few political commentators took Justin Trudeau seriously. "As a rising celebrity aiming to appeal to a generation hungry for entertainment he runs the risk of being treated in a fashion similar to the way other youth celebrities have been treated," observed Stew Slater, the editor of a chain of Ontario regional country newspapers. "It won't be long before his every move is monitored and perhaps not much longer before one of his minor missteps become misconstrued and then magnified a million times by the click of a mouse." Yet like his father, one of the first politicians to use television as a campaign weapon, Justin understood the power of instant media and has never underestimated it. Similarly, the *Globe & Mail* suggested Trudeau needed more seasoning. "To his credit, despite the silly notion being floated that he could be the next Liberal leader he has modestly said he first needs to learn the ropes. I'll say. He may actually have the right stuff, but he needs to demonstrate it convincingly beyond uttering kooky political platitudes and relying on his considerable charm."

The 'silly' notion continued to gather momentum. Writing in the *Regina Leader Post* that summer, Frances Hunter warned that Ignatieff was merely "window dressing," and that it was Justin Trudeau who was being groomed to start a new wave of Trudeaumania in the twenty-first century.

Trudeau wasn't the only one with reservations about Michael Ignatieff. Denis Coderre, the former President of the Queen's Privy Council had concerns of his own. Coderre had supported Ignatieff at the 2006 convention and had become his chief Quebec Lieutenant responsible for assembling star candidates who would run for the Liberals in the forthcoming election. But Coderre found himself increasingly frustrated at being ignored by Ignatieff and by being cut adrift by his team of "Toronto advisors".

Justin Trudeau's stock within the party itself only really began to rise in the summer of 2009. In July he and his brother, Alexandre, went to Memramcork, New Brunswick, for the funeral of former Governor General Romeo Leblanc, a long-time family friend. He walked with Ignatieff in Montreal's Gay Pride Parade, a gesture that Trudeau described as important in the fight for sexual equality. "The Gay and Lesbian community has really suffered for years. They have suffered because of their sexual identity. Today we speak of tolerance, but tolerance is not acceptance," he said. "To tolerate someone is simply to acknowledge they exist and hope they don't come too close to disturb us. Today we have to accept, love and be proud of sexual diversity. Surely we have reached a point in our society where people are able to be themselves and love whomever they want."

In August, he was one of fifteen parliamentarians who went on a training exercise with the Canadian Armed Forces at Camp Wainwright, in Alberta. The Conservatives recognized a growing threat and in September used a Trudeau sound bite taken out of context to undermine his leader, Michael Ignatieff. The interview conducted during the Liberal Leadership convention in 2006 quoted Trudeau as saying, "Ignatieff, he is a little all over the place. He says this, he delivers that, he contradicts himself. Maybe he has the intelligence, but not the wisdom...."

Once again, Trudeau seemed to be everywhere except in the House of Commons. He had become an exponent of 'retail politics' with the voter, selling himself by meeting and talking to as many ordinary Canadians as possible on the streets, schools and shopping malls. It was an exhausting routine of hand shaking, grinning, and stump speaking on the rubber chicken circuit, listening, talking and being photographed close up. As he told the Canadian Press, voters don't pay attention to question period or to parliamentary debates. "Canadians are tuning out. The more we shout louder than everyone so someone will notice, the more people tune us out. They won't listen when you are shouting loud, so let's turn down the volume, let's speak a little softer." It was a touching sign of honesty, and of the younger Trudeau's political integrity.

In addition to his $160,000 MP's salary he was now earning thousands of dollars in public speaking fees, though he is not an orator in the conventional sense of the word. He speaks with a voice that once was compared to "a soothing, warm massage that no one asked for." When he isn't reading from a prepared text or teleprompter his often stilted delivery is often punctuated with a hesitant "Um-uh-uhm," a habit attributed to the fact that he is bilingual, as when he has to think on his feet the brain under pressure has to process not only which word to use but in which language.

He was away from his wife and children so often that rumours began to circulate that Trudeau's marriage was in trouble and, indeed, he and Sophie had agreed to marriage counselling. Trudeau was interviewed on television by Catherine Clark, the daughter of former Prime Minister Joe Clark. During the interview he talked frankly and movingly about how isolated he felt as a Member of Parliament: "It is amazing how lonely a life in Ottawa is. You go home, grab a slice of pizza, make a bowl of cereal, try and watch a little TV and you go to sleep alone and wake up the next morning and go to work." He told Clark how difficult it was for him to leave his wife and two children behind in Montreal each week: "I ask myself is it worth it? So far the work I'm doing, the building that is going on is worth it. The day I think I'm not making much of a difference I'll leave politics."

In October, a major two-volume biography of his father by history professor John English was published. Once again the comparisons between father and son were inevitable.

"It isn't my job to defend my father's record or legacy," he said. "If there is anything I carry forward it's a focus on the strengths and values, his strength of principles, and try to figure out how those values and principles can be articulated today."

That autumn Trudeau was in Kapuskasing in Northern Ontario to meet with area mayors. He talked to the German Club in Brantford, to students at the Brother Andre High School in Markham, to seniors at the Loch Lomond Villa Auditorium in Saint John, New Brunswick. His message was the same: "Our first task is to get Canadians to dream again. It is time to break with the politics of division." He addressed the National Ethic Press and Media Council, a gathering of more than 150 journalists, where again he was asked whether he was positioning himself to lead the party. Again, he was evasive. "I got into politics to make a difference," he replied. "If you spend too much time looking into the future you will trip over things in front of you."

Although he continued to skirt the issue, Justin had long accepted the political advantages of being Pierre Trudeau's son and of how much of an asset he had become to the Liberal party. "All my life I have had people coming at me with certain expectations and certain images. Either you build a wall or you say, 'I'm just me, take it or leave it.' One of two things is going to happen. People will either decide, 'Wow, Justin's changed. He has gotten much more depth and much more serious,' or they will say, 'Maybe we were wrong. Maybe he had it all along.' Bottom line: I don't care, because my story is my story."

He was never allowed to be an ordinary backbench MP. Something as banal as the design of his Christmas card made news. In December his office sent out more than 7,000 greeting cards, 2,000 of them signed in his own hand. When he appeared at the annual Liberal Party Christmas dinner sporting a highland dress kilt he worked the room to great effect. Everyone wanted to see and be seen with the young Trudeau. Even people who didn't like him were anxious to have him pose for selfies. Few were interested in being photographed with Ignatieff. As Chantal Hébert wrote in the *Toronto Star* at the time: "When you think of MPs who arrived on Parliament Hill, more Canadians are aware of Justin Trudeau – though they would be hard pressed to name a single thing he has done – than they are about Conservative cabinet ministers."

Trudeau was one of the first to exploit the subtle gift of new digital technology that was then emerging. Some believe that with each photograph a piece of your soul is stolen and you become part of the world of other people's imaginings. In politics, as with magic, perception is reality. Selfies became a political weapon in Trudeau's arsenal. He intuitively seemed to know what made a good shot, and sometimes directed the camera angles himself. His broad fixed smile was exactly the same in each of the thousands of Trudeau-selfie photographs now circulating on social media. "You figure out early on that perceptions of you can lift you up or bring you down," Trudeau told the *Globe & Mail*. "You have to be true to who you are and hope that that shines through."

During an engagement at McGill University that year,

he met Adam Scotti, the photo editor of the university's newspaper. Justin hired the young photographer – now his official photographer – to take publicity stills on a freelance basis. "His emotive, energetic personality translates especially well visually," explains a former *Toronto Star* photo editor. "He gets in there, he mingles, he is a two-handshake guy. He leans in as if to say 'I hear you', this is our moment." His images are carefully staged to represent public policy, such as welcoming refugees, supporting Gay Pride, or endorsing gender equality. He can be spontaneous in front of the cameras, adapting quickly to unexpected situations. Once on a whim he jumped fully clothed into a swimming pool with his entire family to illustrate a spread for *Chatelaine* Magazine.

As one of his aides put it, "We don't do photo ops, we do symbols – we do image."

CHAPTER NINE

A cataclysmic earthquake in Haiti on 20 January 2010 killed more than 20,000 and left another 1.5 million homeless. About one quarter of Quebec's immigrant population is concentrated in and around Trudeau's Papineau riding and his constituency office moved into high gear to coordinate relief efforts. Trudeau was interviewed on national television by one of his admirers, CTV's Seamus O'Regan, who would later join the Trudeau team. Trudeau took advantage of the interview to urge the Harper government to relax immigration rules in order to allow relatives of Haitian-Canadians to be allowed to come to Canada. "Whether we talk about 1972 and the Ugandan refugees coming over from Idi Amin, whether we talk about '84 and the Ethiopians, whether we talk about Yugoslavians in the '90s, we have welcomed all of those communities in times of crisis," he told O'Regan. "None of them had the advantages of an enormous local population to take them in like the Haitian community [in Papineau]. "

The government's response went beyond party lines. Prime Minister Harper went to Port au Prince to inspect the devastated island and gave priority to immigrants adversely affected, but Trudeau, with his approach to the crisis, gained ground as well.

He spent most of 2010 tagging along at fundraisers with Ignatieff whose lack of leadership skills was becoming more apparent with each passing day. Although the party leader was given top billing as they stumped the country together, the cameras at each event were trained on Trudeau. As one crusty columnist, Allan Fotheringham, remarked, "When Ignatieff smiles, his eyes don't. He can't fake sincerity. If only Justin would grow up faster."

In June, Trudeau was shaken by the news that his former Vancouver roommate Chris Ingvaldson had been arrested and charged with four counts of possession of child pornography. It was especially hard for Trudeau to stomach because Ingvaldson had been largely responsible for getting him his teaching position at West Point Grey Academy. A former field hockey player, Ingvaldson was also preparing to run for the Liberals in Vancouver-Kingsway. Trudeau was totally unaware of his friend's predilections and distanced himself from him quickly. Even before Ingvaldson was convicted and jailed Trudeau publicly disowned their friendship. Aware that he faced a tough battle whenever the Harper minority collapsed and the next election was fought he remained close to his constituency, working the riding for most of the summer, but he was in Baddeck, Nova Scotia for the caucus meeting in July, where he went skinny-dipping.

Ignatieff shuffled his shadow cabinet iSeptember and promoted Trudeau to Opposition Critic for Citizenship and Immigration. Trudeau proved to be effective in the role. In response to the arrival of a shipload of Tamil refugee claimants that summer, Harper's government introduced Bill C-49, a National Action Plan to Prevent Human Smugglers from

Abusing Canada's Immigration System. The government argued that its new rules were necessary to prevent queue-jumpers from gaining entry into Canada. Trudeau made the case that Harper was wilfully exploiting fear and misunderstanding about immigration policy for political gain. Refugees, he pointed out, are not queue-jumpers but asylum seekers "who are fleeing persecution, torture, even threats of death in their home countries, and they are very different from immigrants." Then in the spring of 2011, for the first time in the history of the Commonwealth, Harper's government was found to be in contempt of Parliament. The Commons procedure and House Affairs Committee ruled that the government had failed to disclose its spending priorities. Harper had run out of procedural tricks and could no longer avoid the inevitable. He prepared to face the music. In March, the government fell in a confidence vote, triggering the country's fifth general election in ten years.

Trudeau, fighting to keep his Papineau riding, barely registered in the national campaign that followed. Michael Ignatieff was branded as a crass opportunist, an outsider, someone who "was just visiting." The Conservatives were on a roll. Harper could count on his rural base; all he needed to win a majority was to pick up a dozen seats. Liberals in Quebec who could not bring themselves to vote for Harper and had grave doubts about Ignatieff looked to park their votes with "Smiling Jack Layton." Many liked what Layton was saying – especially disenchanted Quebec nationalists who saw the NDP as a comfortable alternative to the Bloc.

On Election Day, 2 May 2011, Harper increased his popular vote by just two per cent. That was all that was needed to win an additional twenty-four seats, enough at last to give him his majority – 166 seats. He had struggled through three elections in eight years to win his majority but even so, sixty per cent of the Canadian public voted against him. Jack Layton picked up an astonishing fifty-nine seats in Quebec and, with 103 seats, replaced the Liberals as Leader of Her Majesty's Loyal Opposition. The Liberals had expected defeat but no one envisioned the extent of the pummelling they encountered. Ignatieff had led the party to its worst defeat in history. With less than twenty per cent of the vote and only thirty-four seats, Liberals had become a headless body, a leadership without grassroots support. Canada, it seemed, was poised to adopt a two-party system: The Conservatives and the New Democrats. The Liberals had become irrelevant. Or so it seemed. Trudeau lost some votes to the NDP in Papineau but he retained his seat in the House. "We had hoped to do better," said campaign director Denise Handfield, "But I take consolation in the fact that Justin was re-elected."

For Trudeau the election results would prove to be a gift. Ill luck for the Liberals was as much to thank for his political ascendancy as his own skill, inheritance and charm. Not only had he built and expanded his own support base, he had twice won his Papineau riding and proved he could do it without the support of the party's national executive. The party was in disarray. What remained of its leadership was now wary of him. The question was no longer *if* Justin Trudeau would seek the leadership; it was now merely a question of *when*.

After a telephone conference call in June to assess what to do in the aftermath of their shellacking at the polls, Liberals chose Bob Rae as their interim leader and entrusted him to "pull ourselves together" until the party could come to terms with the magnitude of its defeat and hold a leadership convention in 2013.

Official Opposition parties eventually wind up as government but Jack Layton never got his chance to go head to head against Stephen Harper. Layton died of cancer in August, three months after he was sworn in as opposition leader. Thomas Mulcair, the New Democrat from Outremont riding replaced him. Ignatieff resigned in disgrace.

For better or worse, Trudeau continued to dominate the headlines. He had cause to wonder whether he should quit politics altogether and told the *Globe & Mail*'s Sonia Verma he was seriously considering "going somewhere with the wife and kids and raising horses." Again, there is reason to believe that he was sincere – not playing around. At this point, it seemed as if the Liberal Party's part in Canadian politics was over. With only 34 representatives in Parliament, the NDP had replaced them as opposition.

Like his father, Trudeau had little patience with parliamentary rules and procedure. He caused an uproar during question period in December due to an exchange with the environment minister Peter Kent over the Harper government's decision to withdraw from the Kyoto Accord. Sporting a swashbuckler's goatee, Trudeau rejected the minister's explanation with decidedly un-parliamentary language. "Bullshit," he exploded, as he described Kent as "a piece of shit." Then in response to a hypothetical question during a radio interview later that month he put his foot in his mouth again when he declared his support for Quebec independence if the majority of Canadians demonstrated they were in favour of Stephen Harper's social programs. "If I ever believed Canada was really the Canada of Stephen Harper, and was going against abortion, against gay marriage, and going backwards in ten thousand different ways, maybe I would think of wanting to make Quebec a country. If I no longer recognized Canada I would know my own values."

Given his pedigree it is easy to imagine that Justin Trudeau wanted nothing more than to be part of a political dynasty. But like his father Pierre before him, he consistently continued to give the impression that he didn't want to lead the party. Pierre Trudeau had discouraged a political career for his sons and drummed into them the message that anyone who obviously craves political office doesn't deserve it. It was a lesson Justin took to heart. He gave the impression to friends that he really did not want to remain as an MP and went through a period of soul searching. Bob Rae took him out to dinner and encouraged him to stay for the good of the party. In December, Trudeau told a caucus meeting that he would not be a candidate for the leadership. But if he agonized over his future within the party the agony didn't last very long. It was during the Christmas holiday when he turned 41 that he accepted the fact that he had been acclaimed the prince and he agreed to embrace the role and use it to his advantage. His brother, Alexandre, cautioned him against it but even Alexandre recognized that "the movie star politician is a formidable force in this kind of world. Maybe a dangerous one." Having made up his mind to seek the leadership, Justin confided to a friend, "Now I get to play by a different set of rules. I don't have anything to prove."

Margaret Sinclair, Pat Nixon, Justin 1972

Pierre Trudeau 1975

Justin and Sophie arrive at Joint Base Andrews in 2016, the first time for approx. 20 years a Canadian PM visited the White House.

President Barack Obama and First Lady Michelle Obama welcome Prime Minister Justin Trudeau and Mrs Gregoire-Trudeau to the White House, March 2016.

Sophie and Justin 2008

Justin Trudeau at the Regina Boxing Club with former Mayor of Regina, Pat Fiacco. July 2013.

Justin at Pride 2016

Justin Trudeau and Donald Trump, February 2017

Justin and John Kerry

Gerald Butts

Bob Rae

Chrystia Freeland

Jagmeet Singh

Andrew Scheer

Stéphane Dion

Michel Ignatieff

Stephen Harper

The Selfie PM

CHAPTER TEN

Each year since 2006, the Ottawa Regional Cancer Foundation has sponsored "Fight for the Cure," a three-round, celebrity boxing match staged by a private club, Final Round Boxing, to raise money for cancer research. Trudeau saw the event as an opportunity to enhance his reputation nationally and impress voters in his blue collar constituency.

"I was wandering around saying, isn't there a member of the Conservative party who actually wants to punch me in the face? That got me funny looks, but no real takers," he recalled. Until Senator Patrick Brazeau accepted the challenge. Like Trudeau, Brazeau was a dashing figure and like Trudeau, to the camera born. The strapping 37-year-old former model had been national chief of the Congress of Aboriginal Peoples before Prime Minister Harper appointed him to the Senate in 2008. Trudeau accepted the challenge apparently unaware that Brazeau had a black belt in karate. No one thought it was even a remotely good idea. Friends warned Justin not to risk a political future on something as frivolous as a boxing match. "His chances of winning were fifty-fifty," says Serge Joyal. "I warned him that, if he lost, it would really have unfortunate political repercussions. Trudeau left a lot of people shaking their heads and rolling their eyes, but he was determined to roll the dice. He rolled the dice and went for it anyway." As Trudeau later remarked, the fight was a deliberate exercise designed to teach people that he was not someone to be underestimated. He had boxed for 20 years and he believed that the worst case scenario was that, even if Brazeau won, he would remain standing, bloody but unbowed. As he later told *Rolling Stone*, "I wanted someone who would be a good foil, and we stumbled upon the scrappy tough-guy senator from an indigenous community. He fit the bill, and it was a very nice counterpoint. I saw it as the right kind of narrative, the right story to tell."

Promoted as "The Thrill on The Hill," the match in March 2012 took on all the qualities of a medieval trial by combat with Trudeau as the Liberal champion and Brazeau carrying the Conservative colours. The fight was sanctioned by Boxing Ontario using the Olympic rules point system, which meant the boxer who scored the most hits on his opponent would win. It was a real fight. As Brazeau put it: "It's a boxing match, not an aerobics demonstration."

Trudeau trained at least two hours each day several days each week with a well-known professional boxing coach, Charles Nestor, who believes that boxing is as much a mental exercise as it is a physical one. Trudeau was focused. When he learned that Brazeau had not stopped smoking while in training, he was confident that he would be able to wear him out in the ring. Trudeau's brother Alexandre was often his sparring partner. Whatever the consequences, Trudeau was prepared. "If I break my nose, I break my nose," he shrugged. He told *Maclean's* Ashley Geddes that he expected Brazeau to come on very hard, very fast and that in the ring his strategy would be "to keep him at a distance and out think him."

Few thought Trudeau could win. A public opinion poll conducted in mid-March indicated that, nationwide, seventy-three per cent would put their money on Brazeau. Online betting sites gave Brazeau 3 to 1 odds. Trudeau, who stands 6'2", weighed in at 180 pounds; Patrick "Brass Knuckles" Brazeau, at 5'10", was three pounds heavier. In an interview with the CBC's Julie Van Dusen, Trudeau predicted he would win because he was the "smarter" of the two. "Certainly [Brazeau] has gone into this announcing to everyone he is going to win, which means unless he wins decisively and early on, everyone will say 'Oh it was obvious he was going to win,' so he doesn't even win much. I go in as a massive underdog, nobody expects me to do well at all. If I do well, let alone if I win – when I win – everyone will realize that there is a possibility that Justin Trudeau knows what he is doing."

The event was televised live on the now defunct right-wing Sun News Network. Trudeau was bloodied in the first round and appeared to be losing. But he brawled his way through a second and a third round, pounding Brazeau with shots to the head. The referee was forced to stop the fight. Trudeau was declared the winner.

Even he knew his victory was pure luck. "The guy hit me so hard he wobbled my knees. It was a feeling I had never experienced before," he told author Michael Harris. "But my dad taught me to keep throwing punches and that's what I did. At first they missed, then they started landing."

The image of the champ resonated. Trudeau is a huge fan of the *Star Wars* series, and the force was indeed with him.

Everyone was enthralled. He was seen as vulnerable but tough. Like the film hero, Luke Skywalker, he was cool, willing to take risks. He could roll with the punches. He was a winner.

Brazeau was further humiliated and his self-esteem totally demolished when Trudeau took a pair of scissors to his mane of hair in the foyer of the House of Commons while television cameras rolled as Brazeau sported a Team Trudeau T-shirt. You couldn't buy that kind of national publicity. Eager to salvage his and the Conservative party's reputation, Brazeau demanded a rematch. But Trudeau declined. "I won't be fighting boxing matches any more. I have work to do." In fact, Trudeau was already gearing up for something bigger. Much bigger.

Logically, Bob Rae should have been next in line for the party leadership and was encouraged to stand again as a candidate. But the former Ontario Premier had been a two-time contender and had lost both times.

Although Rae wanted to run, the tipping point for him came in June when the party leadership changed the rules to prohibit the interim leader from becoming a leadership candidate. By then, as Rae recalled, it had become apparent that, while Justin gave the impression that he was disinterested in running, a campaign team, with Gerald Butts in charge, was being assembled. "Justin may not have known he was running, but I certainly knew he was," Rae says.

Rae agreed to mind the shop while Trudeau began raising money for his campaign. If Trudeau couldn't pull it off and lead the party to a respectable showing, a merger between the Liberals and the New Democrats seemed inevitable. Liberals had been losing votes in every election since 2000. Quebec, once a party fortress, had been reduced to a toxic wasteland. After the failure of the Charlottetown Accord, the federal Liberals had been mauled in Quebec, first in 1993 by the Bloc Quebecois, then in 2011 by the New Democrats. The patronage scandal and infighting that followed split the forces into two camps, those loyal to Jean Chretien and those loyal to Paul Martin. Many riding associations existed in name only. Justin Trudeau was the party's last, best hope. And he had no intention of being an opposition leader. He was in the ring for the prize.

If Trudeau was to revive the party's fortunes he would have to distance himself from the past to make gains in Ontario, the Maritimes and in British Columbia. He began lining up the help he needed: Tom Pitfield, the son of the former Clerk of the Privy Council Michael Pitfield, was put in in charge of the digital campaign and Pitfield's wife, Anna Gainey, the daughter of a former Montreal Canadiens General Manager, played a senior operations role. Dominic Leblanc, the son of the former Governor General would be the point man in the Maritimes. In Quebec, Trudeau went over the heads of the party hierarchy and recruited Pablo "Hot Rod" Rodriguez, the young Argentine-born communications consultant who had been the Liberal Member of Parliament for the east end Montreal riding of Honore Mercier until his defeat at the hands of the NDP. On the West coast, Bruce Young, a Vancouver-based consultant who got to know Justin when both worked on Gerald

Kennedy's campaign, became part of the campaign team. Trudeau and his young turks were able to mobilize Chretien loyalists who had sat on their hands for two elections, but who now emerged from the woodwork and began organizing for Trudeau. Unlike his father, who did not enjoy having to meet the public, Justin thrived on campaigning. By summer's end it was obvious that wherever he went he resonated with the people who turned out in increasing numbers to meet him. His popularity continued to outstrip the Liberal party brand. The only threat to Trudeau's ambition came from Denis Coderre, a glad-handing politician from another era, who by virtue of his seniority certainly had as good a chance as any to be the next French-speaking leader of the party. Since the days of Sir Wilfrid Laurier the leadership traditionally alternated between French and English. But Coderre had been cut adrift by the party establishment and, like Rae, recognized that he too had been outmanoevered by Trudeau's ground game. He resigned his seat in the House of Commons, forcing an unwanted by-election, and decided instead to run for Mayor of Montreal.

That spring, Trudeau attended a conference in Toronto aimed at "Reviving the Islamic Spirit," and in doing so upset some of his supporters by ignoring the objections voiced by B'nai Brith representatives who were concerned that the meeting had been taken over by Islamist extremists. Trudeau responded to their criticism by saying he supported ethnic unity. He spoke at a gathering in Montreal to mark the centennial of the birth of Irving Layton, a Romanian-born Canadian poet who died in 2006. Trudeau told one of the organizers that he accepted her invitation because he believed in the ability of poets to change the world. He wryly reminded his audience that Layton once referred to his father, Pierre Trudeau, "as a leader worthy of assassination." Then he read one of Layton's poems, 'For the Wife of Mr. Milton'.

His inner circle of trusted advisors from across Canada met at Mont Tremblant in June for a brainstorming session. A number of options were considered, including the idea of a merger with the New Democrats which would unite the left to defeat Harper. They also tossed around the idea of forming a new political party. In the end they reached the conclusion that polticial affiliations are often shaped by factors that have nothing to do with rational deliberation. Many people who stayed away from the polls still identified as Liberal.

Pollsters consistently found that many Liberals had been so turned off by party infighting they no longer bothered to vote, yet they had not abandoned their political beliefs. And the few that did, moved to the right, not to the left. Liberals best represented the status quo, which is why they were described as Canada's natural governing party. Liberals had been in office for two-thirds of the twentieth century. The Liberal brand was strong; it just needed new packaging.

Trudeau's team decided to create a movement with a new mission statement that would rebrand the Liberal name and bring new ideas and new people together. It would be marketed not as a political party per se, but as a grassroots movement. Gerald Butts volunteered to recruit high-profile candidates ("No assholes need apply," he was heard to boast) with the expertise which would allow Justin to develop a broad understanding of issues and public policy that the general public thought were beyond his grasp. A new category of party membership was created to attract non-partisans through a website, Justintrudeau.ca. Joining was as simple as putting an e-mail address on an application form.

That summer, Justin attended the Calgary Stampede with Bob Rae to test the strategy and raise his profile in Alberta. People jumped the queue at the Stampede Breakfast to grab selfies with him in his white ten-gallon Stetson. Asked about when he was to declare his candidacy he remained coy: "I've lived under pressure all my life, I'm very good at handling pressure. You guys will find out by the end of summer, beginning of fall if I've decided and not before."

The announcement, when it came in Ottawa on 2 October, was anti-climactic. He had been on the road campaigning for some time. With the race now officially underway, he disregarded the warning voices of some in his camp and went back to Calgary, a Conservative fortress, to launch his campaign. Nuisance candidates emerged from the woodwork: lawyers David Bertschi and George Takach, a retired Lt. Col in the Canadian Armed Forces, Karen McKrimmon, Former Quebec MP Martin Cauchon, and perhaps the most peculiar of all, constitutional lawyer Deborah Coyne, who was the mother of Justin's half-sister.

None of them were real rivals. What Trudeau needed, in order to show that he himself was credible, was a credible opponent. Astronaut Marc Garneau agreed to make a show of it and enter the race as his stalking horse. Garneau, like Trudeau, had been given short shrift by the party when he first ran for office. He took Westmount in 2008 and, because of NDP leader Jack Layton's personal popularity in Quebec, had come perilously close to losing the seat in 2011 due to the Layton sweep of Quebec. The only others with an outside chance of winning were Vancouver-Quadra MP Joyce Murray and Martha Hall Findlay, a Toronto corporate lawyer and former MP, who had lost her seat in the 2011 election.

Trudeau spent much of the winter of 2012 barnstorming the country. The first indication that he was on to something came during a rally in Jonquiere, a separatist stronghold, where he was not only mobbed by a crowd of teenagers but signed up dozens of new memberships. The same thing happened in Kamloops, a Conservative stronghold, where more than 500 people showed up in a hall that was only big enough for 300. The audiences continued to grow; where hundreds were expected, thousands appeared. "You elected good people to be your voice in Ottawa, but instead you got Stephen Harper's voice," he kept telling them.

For his birthday in December he had a Haida symbol, designed by artist Robert Davidson, *Planet Earth with a Raven*, tattooed on his left arm. In Haida mythology, the raven is a mischievous creature that represents a potent creative force and helps humans achieve their goals. At the time, Davidson said he "felt humoured" by the tattoo. "Traditionally, in Haida culture – and even in modern pop culture – a tattoo is a statement of the values you stand for. Trudeau selected an image depicting one of the origin histories of the Haida nation, where Raven brings light to the world. By selecting that image he must uphold the responsibilities that come with that image. He must bring light to the world. That light cannot be superficial. It must go beyond Trudeaumania and must have substance. It means protecting that which is the source of indigenous cultures – the land and the sea. It means choosing a new path forward from the path of big oil, big industry. Otherwise it is cultural appropriation."

By the time the first leadership debate opened in Vancouver in January 2013 Trudeau was registering 20 times as many 'likes' on Facebook than all his opponents combined. He had 180,000 Twitter followers, Garneau had 10,000. "Justin Trudeau is undeniably the most popular politician in all of Canada," wrote *Maclean's* Jonathan Gatehouse. "A passionate orator and effective advocate for all sorts of causes. The kind of boldface name that can draw packed crowds to liberal fundraisers everywhere."

Even the normally unflappable Stephen Harper seemed spooked by Trudeau's presence in the House of Commons. In their first direct exchange across the aisle in March, Harper twice addressed Trudeau as "the Minister for Papineau," instead of the Honourable Member for Papineau. Trudeau was not yet a Minister of anything, as a mere backbencher, and an opposition one at that – a Freudian slip that left Harper's detractors jeering.

At the Vancouver debate, Trudeau pledged to be the voice of "a powerful middle option" between left and right. His plan, he said, was "to reach out to people across the country who are not polarized, who don't want to vote against something, but want to vote for something." Apart from a promise to legalize marijuana it was hard to tell what his policies were. Joyce Murray based her campaign on the need to reform Canada's electoral system and advanced the notion of preferential ballots to put an end to the current first-past-the-post system of voting.

There were other debates in Winnipeg, Mississaugua and Halifax, but the candidates never really squared off against each other in any of them. Marc Garneau, who had made common cause with Justin, sparred with him in a bad cop-good cop exchange over Justin's failure to enunciate any substantial policies. Garneau warned delegates they could not wait until after the leadership race was over to find out what they signed up for: "That's like asking Canadians to buy a new car without first test-driving it." That allowed Trudeau to reinforce his argument that "you can't win Canadians over with a five point plan. You can't lead from a podium and a press conference. You have to connect with them." The opening allowed Trudeau to emphasise the difference between Liberals and Harper's Conservatives: "Differences of opinion have always been the strength of the Liberal Party. At the end of the day we will be a strong united team ready to face off against Mr Mulcair and Mr Harper."

Garneau withdrew his candidacy as planned, one month before the last debate in Montreal, and threw his support behind Trudeau. Trudeau was guaranteed the prize. But could he lead a party that had been divided, disorganized and demoralized? More to the point, could he defeat Stephen Harper?

While Trudeau was on a flight to Halifax a fellow passenger, Michael Kydd, who worked for the Nova Scotia Progressive Conservatives, slipped him a note and posed the question. Did Trudeau, in all seriousness, really believe he could take on Stephen Harper and win? Trudeau scribbled three words in response: "Just watch me."

In what was now a foregone conclusion, Justin Trudeau was elected leader of the Liberal Party on 14 April 2013 with 77 per cent of the vote. "Canadians turned away from us because we turned away from them," he said in his acceptance speech. "Liberals were more focused on fighting each other than fighting for Canadians. I don't care if you thought my father was great or arrogant. It doesn't matter to me if you were a Chretien Liberal, a Turner Liberal or a Martin Liberal, or any other kind of Liberal. The era of hyphenated Liberals ends now."

Within hours of his victory Conservative attack ads set out to brand the fifth Liberal leader in ten years as being "in way over his head." The television ads featured Trudeau in a tank top doing a strip tease and ridiculed his lack of experience. The voiceover chided him for having been nothing more than "a camp counselor, a white water rafting instructor, a drama teacher for two years and a Member of Parliament with one of the worst attendance records, and now he thinks he can run Canada?"

The campaign failed to register.

Had the Conservatives bothered to run their ads past a non-partisan focus group they would have discovered that Trudeau never appeared more alluring. The image projected was that of an athletic leader who wasn't afraid to do a mock strip tease for charity. A white water rafting instructor was certainly not something to be ashamed of, certainly not in Canada. And as for being a drama teacher, that was not something to be disparaged either. In the week after the attack ads were aired, the Liberals gained three points in the public opinion polls and the party raised $500,000. The ads backfired. Even a grade five class in Ottawa wrote to the Prime Minister's Office asking Harper not to be so mean to Justin Trudeau.

By then, however, Harper's office had more than Trudeau to worry about. Three of the Prime Minister's recent star appointees to the Senate had become embroiled in a scandal involving their expense accounts. Mike Duffy was accused of defrauding the Senate of $90,000, Pamela Wallin, a television producer and former Canadian consul-general to New York, of $150,000, and Patrick Brazeau of $50,000.

Timing in politics is everything. Justin Trudeau assumed the leadership at the very moment that the growing rot that infected the Harper government was about to be exposed. In May, CTV's Robert Fife reported that the RCMP had launched an investigation into charges of corruption in the Prime Minister's Office itself after the Mounties had learned that Harper's chief of staff, Nigel Wright, had written a personal cheque to cover Duffy's expenses in an attempt to put a lid on the emerging fraudulent expense account scandal.

CHAPTER ELEVEN

Each spring, Parliament Hill in Ottawa was sweet with the scent of marijuana as thousands of demonstrators in favour of legalizing cannabis staged a countercultural smoke-in. Soon after winning the leadership Trudeau declared that his position on the subject had evolved. He had been in favour of decriminalization as "a great first step" but now had come around to the view that pot was "no worse than cigarettes or alcohol."

What he didn't mention was that shortly before his brother had been killed in the avalanche, Michel had been charged with simple possession and that his mother, Margaret, too, had once been charged with possession in 1988, and in her 60s still lights up. She sees pot as "the occasional glass of wine... I like the way I suddenly notice the colour of my flowers, the way I see the moon with fresh eyes. My imagination becomes more vivid and active and I feel happy."

Trudeau also casually mentioned that he himself had smoked pot "five or six times" in his life, including once since he had been elected to Parliament.

"I do not consume cannabis. I am not a consumer, but I have tried it," he confessed. "I've never been a user of marijuana to any large degree. But we are going to have to have a serious policy discussion about change because the current approach isn't working. We have an awful lot of support from people, and we have the facts and figures to back it up. I am serious about taking on a different approach to the failed war on drugs."

Opposition reaction was predictable. "It is against the law to smoke dope," Justice Minister Peter MacKay reminded Trudeau. "Most Canadians expect their member of Parliament to obey the law." As it turned out, most Canadians didn't object to Trudeau's toking. As scores of other parliamentarians across the country, including Ontario's premier and Toronto Mayor Rob Ford, admitted they had also inhaled in their lifetimes, support for legalization could be found in some of the least expected places. "He is the only elected official in Canada able to get away with it. His appeal is tremendous and his ideas are fresh," Chris McKerracher wrote in the conservative Wetaskawin, Alberta *Pipeline Flyer*. "You may not agree with what he says, but his name is on the lips of the folks in the taverns, coffee shops and around office water coolers across the land."

Concerned about the attention Trudeau was getting, Harper's office sent out a six page memo just before the Liberal Policy Convention opened in Montreal in August 2013 urging its members to troll social media to "fan the flames of Liberal infighting" and to troll websites to portray Trudeau as inept.

Once again, Trudeau had another card up his sleeve to deflect the negative vibes. His wife Sophie wasn't with him at the convention, but she appeared to delegates via Skype to explain why. "I can't join you tonight physically, but it is an honour to be joining you like this," she cooed as she stood before the cameras to reveal that she was two months pregnant with their third child. (The Trudeaus' son was born in 2014 and named Hadrien. If he is indeed named for the Roman Emperor Hadrian – notice the difference in spelling – his name honours the warrior who built a wall to keep the Scots out of Britannia, brutally crushed a Jewish uprising in 133 and elevated his lover, Antinous, to the status of a god after the teenager drowned.)

The Senate expense account scandal continued to percolate throughout the summer. Attempts by the Prime Minister's Office to force Duffy, Brazeau and Wallin out of the Red Chamber failed. By design, Canadian Senators, in theory, have as much power as a member of Parliament, and can do pretty much what they want to do except originate money bills. The Senate operated under its own rules and policed its own budget. Expense claims were often routinely approved without documentation. Senators like Duffy, Brazeau and Wallin, who believed themselves "entitled to their entitlements" dug in their heels and contested the claims.

In August, Trudeau marched in the Gay Pride parade in Montreal, then turned up on the other side of the country in Haida Gwaii to raise a totem pole. He donned a Jalabiya and went to worship with Muslims in the Jamaia Musjid Mosque.

He met with Quebec Premier Pauline Marois in Quebec City to register his disapproval of the PQ government's proposed Charter of Quebec Values, which would bar provincial government employees from wearing religious symbols such as crucifixes, stars of David, turbans, niqabs, hijabs and kippas. Trudeau castigated Marois's minority government for planting the seeds of division with its proposed legislation. "Our job is social inclusion, our job is making all groups who come to this country, whatever their race, ethnicity or religion, feel at home. That is our job."

By the time the Liberal caucus met in Prince Edward Island at the end of the summer, Justin Trudeau's approval rating was the highest of any of the three political leaders in Canada. When pressed for details about his party's plans, Trudeau was extremely vague. He allowed that he had an "awful lot of hard work" ahead of him if he was to rebuild "the third party" before the election. He cleverly changed the narrative and suggested that the Conservatives had become the party of the elite and that he alone was the champion of the middle class. It became the movement's catch phrase.

"My responsibility is to put forward a comprehensive, robust platform in 2015 that is going to demonstrate that the Liberal party is serious about working to improve conditions for the middle class, and I am not going to short-cut that process just because people are impatient and want to know right now."

Relations between Canada and the United States had deteriorated during the Harper years, in part over Harper's aggressive support for a proposed $10 billion Keystone XL Pipeline designed to ship bitumen from Alberta through the United States to be refined in Texas. Harper pushed the plan; President Barack Obama, citing environmental concerns, vetoed the scheme. Harper then came up with an alternative idea that would see the oil piped across British Columbia through a Northern Gateway pipeline, and on to China, which raised the ire of environmentalists and First Nations along the West Coast. No relationship is as crucial to Canada as its dealings with the United States; 75 per cent of Canada's export trade is with the United States, and Canada is the best customer for imports from 35 key states. Although reduced to third party status, the Liberals still had allies in Washington where Trudeau made the obligatory visit to outline his balanced approach to trade relations and to lobby in favour of the Keystone XL Pipeline. He followed up the trip to the United States with a carefully timed speech to the Petroleum Club in Calgary on the eve of a Conservatives Convention being held in the city.

The Trudeau name was anathema in Alberta ever since Pierre Trudeau introduced a National Energy Policy to regulate the petroleum industry by taxing all oil refined in Canada. The agreement, designed to benefit consumers in Eastern Canada, eventually cost Alberta billions of dollars. Well aware that Calgary was hostile territory, the new leader set out to mend fences. "This place is important: Calgary, Alberta, and all of Western Canada. It's important now, and it will be even more important in the future – our shared future. Those of us who aspire to positions of national leadership need to get that, or we will never truly be national leaders," he assured the sceptical oil barons. In spite of environmental concerns, he outlined an approach to energy development which was the same as Harper's in theory, but more nuanced in practice. Having examined the facts and accepting the judgement of the National Energy Board, he said he supported Keystone: "It would create jobs and growth, strengthen our ties with the world's most important market, and generate wealth. Most of all it is in keeping with what I believe is a fundamental role of the Government of Canada: to open up markets abroad for Canadian resources and to help create responsible and sustainable ways to get those resources to those markets."

As the transition from Member of Parliament to Party Leader consumed more of his time in Ottawa, he sold his house in Outremont and moved his family into a six bedroom Georgian mansion that he rented in Ottawa's Rockcliffe Park neighbourhood.

Justin Trudeau didn't generate the same level of Trudeaumania that his father, Pierre, had in the 1960s, but he was attracting the kind of serious attention that began to worry Harper. Veteran political observer Chantal Hébert put her finger on the mood afoot when she wrote: "No other leader in my experience has been on the receiving end of so much early interest. By and large, the curiosity I encountered was almost equally devoid of hostility and passion. It was often laced with a healthy dose of scepticism. But the scepticism seemed to decrease over the long months that Trudeau has just spent under the microscope, but some of it lingers… whether voters are becoming increasingly comfortable with Trudeau over the course of his transition from political rock star to third party leader, or increasingly indifferent as the novelty wears off is a question that four by-elections later this fall will begin to answer."

The results of the by-elections in November confirmed Hébert's opinion. Canadians were beginning to warm to Trudeau. Although, as expected, the Conservatives held on to the two seats up for grabs in their western Canadian heartland. The Liberal popular vote increased in Manitoba by 37 per cent in Brandon and went up by 23 per cent in Provencher. In Toronto, Chrystia Freeland, the Harvard graduate and Rhodes scholar who speaks five languages and who had been persuaded to give up a job as managing editor with Thomson-Reuters in New York to run for the Liberals, won with 50 per cent of the vote. Even in Quebec the candidate in Bourassa, Denis Coderre's old riding, increased the Liberal vote by seven per cent. Freeland was an especially impressive recruit; she had run the *Financial Times* Moscow bureau where she became well connected in Russian circles.

The Throne Speech that fall marked the unofficial start of the federal election campaign. The next episode in the Senate scandal came in November when the three Conservative senators were suspended without pay for "gross negligence" for inappropriate billing of their travel and living expenses and the stain began to spread into the Liberal camp when an investigation into the spending habits of one of their own senators, Marc Harb, was announced. Trudeau claimed that Harb "misunderstood the rules," and would welcome him to caucus until the matter was resolved. But Harb resigned in August and reimbursed the Senate $230,000. Five months later, as a growing number of senators on both sides of the house faced criminal charges over the misuse of public funds, Trudeau would demonstrate a ruthless approach. He turned his back on long-time loyalists in the Upper House and distanced himself from the growing spending scandal. In a daring and unprecedented move in January 2014, Trudeau expelled the thirty-two Liberal senators from caucus. Every one of them.

"The Senate is broken and needs to be fixed," he explained. Claiming to be a "relentless reformer" Trudeau promised he would take "bold steps" to reform the Senate and "build public institutions that Canadians can trust." He hoped that divorcing the party from Senate appointees would put an end to patronage. By being separate from political or electoral concerns, he argued independent senators would be able to do what was best for their country or region, not what was in the party's best interest. "That is why I have come to believe that the Senate must be non-partisan," he declared.

As his confidence grew, so too did signs of his high-handedness. In May he announced that, in spite of his assurances that the party would hold open nomination meetings, prospective candidates would be screened and those who supported the pro-life option would be prohibited from being a candidate. It included those sitting members in his caucus who were against abortion. A politician's duty, he pointed out, was to uphold the Canadian Charter of Rights and Freedoms, not the tenets of any one religion.

"The days when old men get to declare what a woman does with her body are long gone," he tweeted. In defending his position he cited a quote attributed to Oliver Wendell Holmes: "Your right to swing your arm ends where my nose begins. When we are balancing a woman's right to do what she wants to her own body with legislation that restricts that right you are not defending women's rights," he argued. "That doesn't mean people can't be against abortion in their personal views, but if you want to be a Liberal MP you can't vote to limit women's rights." One former MP, a staunch Roman Catholic, Clifford Lincoln, found it extremely ironic that a party that called itself Liberal would prohibit a dissenting opinion on any issue. "I find it very, very sad for a leader to issue an edict which subscribes to only one set of values. Surely as parliamentarians we deal with this in caucus, and respect one another's views and convictions." Other party officials were genuinely puzzled by the dogmatic position. "No one at the top or at the party level other than Justin's sycophants believe he has two stones to rub together. He has created an issue where there was no issue." But critics who complained were yesterday's men.

Perhaps nothing that Steven Harper did as Prime Minister damaged his reputation more than his malicious and unfounded attack that month on Canada's female Chief Justice Beverley McLaughlin. The Supreme Court had ruled that one of Harper's choices was ineligible to sit on the High Court because he did not meet regional residency requirements. Infuriated, the Prime Minister not only accused McLaughlin of meddling in the decision to block the judge, but he also threatened to amend the Supreme Court Act to overrule the supremacy of the Canadian constitution and bend the court to his will.

While Trudeau was in Winnipeg en route to a summer caucus meeting in Edmonton, a drunk 19-year-old broke into his house in Rockcliffe while Sophie and the children were asleep upstairs. It was an unnerving incident, but the intoxicated young man had left a note of "apology and remorse" behind and no charges were ever laid. The episode raised concerns about security, but as the leader of a rump party in Parliament, he wasn't entitled to police protection.

The first major foreign policy issue to confront Trudeau as party leader was the government's decision to deploy six CF-18 fighter jets to help the international coalition against ISIS. Speaking against the motion, Marc Garneau outlined the party's position in a persuasive speech which suggested Canada should instead provide "a military role of a non-combat nature," offering humanitarian aid while other countries conducted the air strikes. Trudeau, in an off-the-cuff remark on television, blew it. Resorting to sophomoric phallic humour, he rejected the government's reasoning: "Why aren't we talking more about the kind of humanitarian aid that Canada can and must be engaged in, rather than, you know, trying to whip out our CF-18s and show them how big they are? It just doesn't work like that in Canada."

It was an embarrassing remark that didn't sit well with critics, who ridiculed Trudeau's reaction to a legitimate question as immature and described him as a "jellyfish in search of a backbone."

One week later, on 22 October, as the Liberals prepared for a caucus meeting in the Centre Block, a deranged gunman went on a rampage in the Hall of Honour one floor above their meeting room. Trudeau and a number of government employees were herded into another committee room where he calmly took charge and helped ease the hysteria. He chatted to a construction worker about renovations being done to the West Block and asked whether he might tour the site. "Sure, but you will have to give my boss your name," the worker replied.

After a nine-hour lockdown ending in the terrorist's death Trudeau emerged apparently unperturbed. "Criminals will not dictate to us how we act as a nation, how we govern ourselves or how we treat each other," he said and reassured Muslims "that acts such as these committed in the name of Islam are an aberration of your faith. We will walk forward together, not apart." The contrast between Stephen Harper, who hid in a closet during the attack (wisely, one may add, under the circumstances), and Trudeau, who appeared to have mustered courage and shown backbone in the face of danger, could not be more obvious.

Trudeau's strength, in the words of one long-time Liberal organizer was that he was "threateningly young." It was obvious that his appeal was widespread and that a whole new generation was ready to follow him and take over. "He was what was happening. If the old party hacks are smart, and really want to win, they had best just get out of the way and let him do it."

A romantic, Arthurian aura enveloped him; he was now Galahad, Lancelot and Arthur all rolled into one. As one partisan gushed after meeting him: "This is the man we expect to pull the sword from the stone."

Among the tools Trudeau's movement had at its disposal was a sophisticated computer program known as "The Console," which had been developed by strategists at party headquarters. It broke down Canada's 338 electoral ridings into six categories: platinum, gold, silver, bronze, steel and wood. Platinum ridings were safe Liberal seats. There weren't many of those. Gold were identified as the ridings the party could regain with hard work, silver were pure toss ups, steel were marginal, and wood – most of them in the prairie provinces – were considered a total write-off. There was no ground game in Quebec. The state-of-the-art machine gathered information from volunteers, who went door-to-door canvassing voters and matched it with historical data, demographic trends and evaluated the three party leaders. Trudeau had an unusually high recognition factor. His role now was to connect with the voters, to get volunteers to draw people in and get them on stream.

Stephen Harper would campaign on his economic record, and remind Canadians of how well his government had managed the economy; Trudeau had a clear vision of the campaign ahead and a realistic strategy for winning it. Trudeau would beat the drum for the middle class and capitalize on his personal popularity and meet one-to-one with as many people as possible. He played it masterfully. The movement became a slick marketing franchise selling memberships, T-shirts, commemorative mugs, limited edition Justin Trudeau scarves and memorabilia. There were e-mails from Justin urging friends to "show leadership by example by chipping in $5 right now to help drive the movement." Hell, you could even win a dinner date with the guy. Within eighteen months, party membership went up almost 250 per cent from 60,000 to 300,000.

CHAPTER TWELVE

The defection of Eve Adams, the Conservative member for Mississauga-Brampton South, to the Liberal benches in February 2015 proved to be a double-edged sword for Trudeau. Adams was young and had been a parliamentary secretary in Harper's government, but she was no prize catch. Having lost her riding through re-distribution, the Conservatives washed their hands of her after it was learned that her fiancé, Dimitri Soudas, who happened to be the executive director of the Conservative Party of Canada, had illegally tried to rig a nomination meeting in another riding in her favour. Soudas was fired and Adams was banned from running as a Conservative in the forthcoming election. Having no other prospects, she badmouthed Harper as being "mean-spirited" and joined the Liberals. Without consulting his caucus, and ignoring the backlash from his supporters, Trudeau welcomed the belligerent carpetbagger with open arms into his "movement."

Secure in the knowledge that, without any organization or connections Adams would never win an open nomination as a Liberal in any riding, Trudeau paraded her to his advantage. Her defection, he said, served to showcase his ability to bring together "people of all different political stripes." Trudeau recognizes sycophants; if he embraces one it is to advance his own agenda. Once they are no longer useful to him, they are disposed of. The political benefits of accepting Adams into caucus were immediate and outweighed any criticism from his supporters that he had shown a lack of judgement. It was good political theatre. Six months later, Adams lost the fight for the nomination to represent the Liberals in Toronto-Eglington riding and hasn't been heard from since. Trudeau also demonstrated his zero tolerance for anyone who might tarnish the Liberal brand with even a hint of misconduct. Two Liberal MPs who were rumoured to be guilty of inappropriate behaviour – Scott Andrews, who represented Newfoundland-Labrador, and Massimo Pacetti, the MP for St. Leonard St-Michel – learned from television reports that Trudeau had removed them from caucus without even bothering to meet with them because allegations of sexual misconduct had been levelled against them. Neither man was ever charged, but their political careers were over.

Trudeau's mother, Margaret, published another memoir, *Changing My Mind*, and on the promotion tour she used the opportunity to promote her son as well. As far as Margaret was concerned it was never a question of "if" Justin would become Prime Minister, but "when." Privately, she told friends she was confident he would win a majority. Although she didn't hit the campaign trail, she never ducked the question if asked. "What Justin is offering is the alternative to a sort of non-transparent, manipulative, backstabbing kind of politics," she told one interviewer. "Justin wants to change that and I hope he can. I don't know if he can because politics is a really fine-tuned game if you know it well."

When Parliament resumed, Harper introduced Bill C-51, legislation designed to "stand up to Jihadists," to fight against ISIS and protect the safety and security of Canadians. Trudeau was critical of the bill but voted for it anyway, promising to amend its provisions if he was elected Prime Minister. In a speech to McGill University alumni in Toronto, he described the legislation as written as a "threat to liberty.":

> It stokes anxiety and it foments fear. Instead of encouraging Canadians to fight for one another's liberty, it tells us to be suspicious of each other's choices. In defending Canada we cannot allow ourselves to be less Canadian.

The Harper government's boast that it had managed the economy well was compromised by a significant drop in oil prices, which forced the budget to be postponed. Once it was brought down in March, the Liberals announced the centrepiece of what would be their campaign when Trudeau unveiled his program to help the elusive, undefined 'middle class.' It was an appealing sentiment to at least the 50 per cent of the country that considered itself middle class, whether they had annual incomes of $50,000 or $150,000. Then in June, Liberals amplified their pitch to voters with a 32-point election program that pledged "to improve the way Canadians vote, improve how government serves you and ensure that Parliament is more than just the Prime Minister's rubber stamp."

Trudeau wasn't especially enthusiastic about electoral reform but, facing pressure from both the NDP and members of his own caucus, he promised to introduce legislation that would change the way Canadians vote within 18 months of forming a government. Personally, he favoured the two-round system used in French presidential elections, in which voters rank their first, second and third choices. If no candidate receives an absolute majority on the first ballot, the last place candidate is dropped and a run-off is held. He also pledged that his cabinet would have an equal number of men and women.

Trudeau was in Vancouver for the Gay Pride parade on August 2 when Prime Minister Harper kicked off an ill-advised eleven-week election campaign. The 78-day campaign would be the longest since 1872 and would include five televised debates. What Harper failed to recognize is that it is television that tends to help get people elected. Trudeau was to the camera born. One of his parlour tricks, which he cheerfully demonstrated on television, was to fall down a flight of stairs without hurting himself. It was the kind of thing that had people talking and revealed the sharp contrast between the risk-taking, fun-loving Trudeau and Harper's severe image. Juvenile behaviour or not, it had people talking.

The longer an election campaign, the more fraught with danger it becomes for all parties involved. Harper was confident that his record of sound economic management of a trillion dollar economy alone would carry him to a fourth mandate. He gambled that a long campaign would exhaust the NDP's resources and at the same time demonstrate, as the

Conservative campaign ads constantly reminded the public, that Justin "was just not ready."

Harper was at a disadvantage: his government had been around for almost ten years. He had become, in the words of his sympathetic biographer John Ibbitson, "Autocratic. Secretive. Cruel." As Ibbitson wrote, "There has never been a Prime Minister as utterly contemptuous of people outside his voting coalition as Stephen Harper."

Canada was headed for a recession and Harper's Minister of Finance, Jim Flaherty, who had indeed managed the Canadian economy well, had died in April 2014. In addition, any notion that the Duffy affair had been swept under the rug disappeared when the senator's trial on 31 counts of fraud, breach of trust and bribery resumed on August 12. Testimony during the trial again exposed the inner workings of the Prime Minister's Office and served as a daily reminder of Harper's lack of judgement.

Harper tried to ignore the criminal proceedings against one of his key appointees by reminding voters that his role was "not to apologize for the bad activities of others; the role of a leader is to hold people accountable, and that is what we are doing." But the daily accounts of the trial kept Harper off message.

Curiously, it was Trudeau, not Mulcair, who was perceived as the main threat to Harper when the Conservatives launched their first attack ads. The 60-second spot depicted an employee selection committee sitting around a boardroom table, assessing Trudeau's application for the job. One of the participants points out that being Prime Minister is "not an entry level job." Another agrees that "he has some growing up to do." But one member of the selection committee undermines the whole negative premise by acknowledging Trudeau's potential: "I'm not saying no this time, maybe next time." The kicker, "Nice hair though," which was meant to ridicule Trudeau, in fact reminded voters, if they needed any reminding, that he was handsome and not *all* that stupid. While the ad set out to paint Trudeau as someone who wasn't ready, it conveyed a subliminal message: in a field of applicants he was an attractive candidate with little experience who might one day be worthy of consideration. The eleven-week campaign would allow plenty of time for the public to accept the princeling as a leader.

Harper also misread public opinion by waging a tough on crime campaign. He took aim at Trudeau as a "reckless politician that would condone or normalize the use of illegal drugs," but Canadians overwhelmingly supported the legalization of pot.

All indicators in the first weeks of the campaign showed the New Democrats pulling ahead of the Conservatives. The election of an NDP government five months earlier in Alberta which unexpectedly ended 44 years of Conservative rule in the western province invigorated Mulcair's campaign team. There, feeling was widespread that the momentum dubbed "the orange wave," that swept the party to unprecedented victories in Quebec and now in Alberta, would flood the country and carry the NDP to victory.

The simple truth, however, was that the NDP's war room had neither the resources nor the backroom expertise needed to wage an eleven-week election battle on a national scale.

The narrative on the hustings began to change in early September with the death of Alan Kurdi, a three-year-old Syrian refugee in the far off Mediterranean. Kurdi drowned with his mother and brother as the family was attempting to make its way to Vancouver. Images of the boy's body washed up on the beach near Bodrum galvanized the world. Then there were revelations that the Harper government had rejected the family's privately sponsored application for landed immigrant status. Harper's measured response to the situation seemed to be devoid of all empathy. The boy, he said, was but one of thousands of innocent victims of the war. He rejected the notion that changes to Canada's immigration policy could alone solve the refugee crisis. He suggested instead that increased military action was needed to prevent ISIS from killing tens of millions of people: "I don't know how for the life of me you can look at that picture and you say, 'yeah we want to help that family but we want to walk away from the military mission.'"

Although Harper had promised to accept 10,000 Syrian refugees, under intense media scrutiny it turned out that in fact only 1,000 applications had been processed. Trudeau promised that if elected he would accept 25,000 Syrian refugees.

As the refugee crisis dominated the campaign, the Liberals released a simple but effective television ad which showed Trudeau walking up a down escalator, getting nowhere. It served to drive home the message that in eight years of Harper government, middle class Canadians had not been able to get ahead.

The whole campaign turned when "fear of the other" became the overriding issue. On September 15, a federal appeal court ruled that a woman had a right to wear a niqab when she took the Canadian citizenship oath. The court ruling was extremely unpopular in Quebec, which was grappling with cultural differences and with the whole issue of what constitutes reasonable accommodation. Mulcair defended the court's decision on face coverings even though he knew it would be anathema in Quebec, where the party had most of its seats. "I understand that many view the niqab as a symbol of oppression of women. And on that let me be clear. No one has the right to tell a woman what she must — or must not wear. But if some of these women are being oppressed, we have to reach out to them, not deprive them of their Canadian citizenship."

That played into the hands of Harper's campaign. Mulcair had earlier denounced Bill C-51 as "sweeping, dangerously vague and ineffective," and because he supported the niqab, the Conservatives were quick to paint him as soft on terrorism.

Trudeau had supported the anti-terrorist legislation but, recognising the hostility to its draconian provisions, he now disingenuously promised to repeal its "problematic elements" and limit some of its powers if he was elected. He sidestepped the niqab issue saying the court had spoken and blamed Harper for creating a wedge issue by creating a problem where none existed.

According to John Doyle, the country's eminent television critic, the turning point in the campaign came in mid-September, when the three party leaders were in Iqaluit, Nunavut, in Canada's high Arctic.

It all had to do with image.

"Harper looked awkward in an ill-fitted padded jacket over his suit jacket and pants. Tom Mulcair was in Iqaluit too, equally underdressed in a sport jacket and sweater. Trudeau looked utterly at home there," Doyle wrote in the *Globe & Mail*. "He's in jeans, knee high boots, and a waist length parka worn open. He's got one of his children tucked under his left arm. He projected youth, strength, vitality and, more importantly, blithe confidence. That is a core aspect of character that simply cannot be faked."

By then, swing voters who didn't like Harper and no longer warmed to Mulcair began to take a second look at Trudeau. They didn't dislike what they saw. Liberals had been gaining a percentage point each week since the start of the campaign. Mulcair added to his predicament when he promised to balance the budget. During the debate in Calgary on the economy Trudeau said a Liberal government was prepared to run "modest deficits," no more than $10 billion a year, to fund infrastructure spending. He also promised a balanced budget by 2019.

With that a group of influential NDP supporters sabotaged Mulcair's moderate, middle-of-the-road campaign by demanding a hard turn to the left. The group unveiled its own extreme Leap Manifesto, which called for an end to fossil fuel subsidies, increased corporate taxes and the introduction of a carbon tax, arguing that the party had become so pre-occupied with its polling numbers that it had abandoned its mission "to overhaul the capitalist system."

The panic among the rank and file in the NDP was evident, no more so than in Trudeau's own riding of Papineau, where the NDP released the laughable results of a poll that claimed that its candidate, Montreal broadcaster Anne Legace Dowson, was running well ahead of the Liberal leader. The poll proved to be fraudulent. No one believed it. By the ninth week the NDP campaign was in meltdown. Harper's campaign, too, began to come apart at the seams when it was learned that it had invited Australian political strategist Lynton Crosby, known in political circles as "the Wizard of Oz," to help turn the Conservative campaign around. Crosby had helped David Cameron's campaign in Britain, and is credited with getting Boris Johnson elected mayor of London. Bringing Crosby in at the last minute smacked of desperation.

In the final leaders' debate conducted in French in Montreal on October 2 Trudeau was subdued. The worst that could be said about his performance came from political science professor Guy Lachapelle who complained that "his thoughts are not organized in a francophone way."

Then, at the rally in Brampton, Ontario on October 5, Trudeau emerged with all barrels blazing. In a nationally televised barnburner of a speech he railed against Harper as "small, meek and fearful," pointing out that the Prime Minister had fought eight elections and was asking for a fourth term. "It's like a bad movie franchise, most of the stars are gone, and the plot is getting pretty thin." Trudeau was careful not to alienate Harper's supporters. "Conservatives are not our enemies. They're our neighbours. They want what is best for their country, just like we do," he insisted. "We don't need to convince them to leave the Conservative party. We just need to show how Stephen Harper's party has left them."

Within days of that speech, the Liberal lead increased. By the tenth week of the campaign, four pollsters – Nanos, Leger, Ekos and Mainstreet – had Trudeau in a statistical tie with Harper. So uncertain was the outcome, that Governor General David Johnston's term in office was extended in case the results provoked a constitutional crisis. It would appear that the die was cast during the Canadian Thanksgiving Day weekend in October when many families across the land sat down to their turkey dinners and considered the options of strategic voting. The *National Post's* Chris Selley distilled the political transformation taking place: "Mulcair was a Liberal in drag, he is Justin Trudeau without the smile, who in turn is Stephen Harper *with* a smile."

Harper didn't do himself or the party any favours in the dying days when he showed up at a rally with Toronto's internationally disgraced cocaine-sniffing, crack-smoking mayor Rob Ford. The traditionally conservative newspaper *The Globe & Mail* then ran what can only be described as a bizarre, back-handed editorial endorsement: *The Tories, an Imperfect Choice.* ("What Canada needs is a Conservative government that is no longer the Harper government. [Harper's] party deserves to be re-elected, but after Oct. 19, he should quickly resign.)

In simplest terms, by the time the campaign moved towards its climax, Harper was perceived to be sneaky, mean and vindictive; Mulcair's every smile now seemed to be an evil grimace. It was Trudeau who was the most vigorous and energetic, the leader who offered a compassionate "sunny" vision of the Canadian ideal. And he was attractive to boot. He *did* have nice hair. One week before the election, the Liberals surged past the NDP in the public opinion polls. At a rally in Nepean Trudeau took advantage of the soundings to drive home the message that the NDP were out of the race, and that the Conservatives were no longer fit to govern:

> We are on the verge of something special. We have a chance to prove that fear and division won't work here, not in Canada. We have the chance to replace a vision of this country that is small and mean and nasty with a vision that is confident, optimistic and positive. Canada is a great country because we look at diversity and differences as a source of strength, of resilience within our communities. We are there for each other as a country. And when Mr Harper chooses to exploit those differences for political gain, we start turning away from what has made Canada successful, our openness, our understanding, our generosity.

By election day pollsters were certain of one thing: a minority government. But no one dared predict whether it would be a Trudeau or Harper minority.

Trudeau sucked on a beer in his suite in the Fairmont Queen Elizabeth Hotel in Montreal on election night as he and about twenty of his friends watched the early returns come in from the East Coast. Two Conservative cabinet ministers were swept away in a rising red tide as the Liberals took every one of the 32 seats in the four Atlantic provinces. To his satisfaction he began to pick up more seats in Quebec than had been expected to – 40 of the 78 seats – the Liberals' best showing in that province in 35 years. By the time the results from Ontario trickled in he was already elected or leading in 80 ridings. There was little doubt that he would be the next Prime Minister of Canada. He gained two seats in Calgary, the first Liberal MPs to be elected from the Conservative heartland in almost 50 years, and two more in Edmonton. The Calgary wins were especially historic – Kent Hehr, a 45-year-old lawyer who took Calgary Centre, had been paralyzed in a drive-by shooting when he was 21 years old and Dashan Singh Kahn, who took Calgary Skyview, had come to Canada from India in 1970.

Gerry Butts and his campaign team had indeed tapped into the mood of the electorate. Trudeau had not only galvanized the youth vote but made headway into aboriginal communities, which rarely vote in federal elections. Turnout of those between the ages of 18 to 24 rose to 57 per cent from 38.8 per cent in 2011. The First Nations vote went up by 17 per cent.

When the smoke cleared, Trudeau's candidates had won 184 seats, 84 of them represented by women. It was the largest comeback of any political party in Canadian history.

Trudeau didn't get much sleep that night. The next morning at dawn he breezed into the Jarry Metro station to be with his own constituents in his Papineau riding. He hugged well-wishers, had selfies snapped with them and shook hands even with those who didn't vote for him.

His handlers, well aware of the impression the exposure would make, made sure television cameras from the various networks were on hand to record the Prime Minister elect's 'spontaneous' gesture. The international press had a field day. "Canada's new Prime Minister is so bangable Americans might start caring about Canadian politics," exclaimed one US website. The popular E! Online website declared Trudeau to be "smoking hot, a syrupy fox." And in the UK *The Daily Mirror* asked, "Is Justin Trudeau the sexiest politician in the world?"

CHAPTER THIRTEEN

It wasn't until after he had sworn the oath of office and strode past the Prime Ministers' Portrait Gallery in Parliament's Centre Block that the impact of the transfer of power really hit home. When Myfanwy Pavelic's official portrait of his father wearing a loden cape with a red rose in the lapel caught his eye, he visibly choked. He was there for the unveiling and had walked past the painting many times as an MP and had seen the image reproduced on a commemorative postage stamp. But now it dawned on him that his portrait too would one day also hang in the same corridor along with that of his father's and the twenty-two other Prime Ministers of Canada. He was no longer the little boy playing hide and seek with his brothers on the third floor of the Centre Block outside his father's parliamentary office. He was Prime Minister on his way to the same office his father had once occupied.

The full gravity of the occasion fell on him.

Trudeau unveiled a youthful cabinet of fifteen men and fifteen women "that looks like Canada." In addition to regional balance, the ministry reflected gender equality, ethnic diversity, and youth. It included an Inuit (Hunter Too Too), an aboriginal (Jody Wilson-Raybould), two Sikhs (Navdeep Bains and Bardish Chagger), a Muslim (Maryam Monsef), and a Jew (James Carr). Only a third of his ministers – like Stéphane Dion, Marc Garneau, Ralph Goodale and John Mc-Callum – had previous experience. Bill Morneau, the president of Morneau-Shepell, one of the country's biggest pensions and benefits companies, who had been a pension investment advisor to the Ontario government, was tapped as Minister of Finance. By appointing 15 women to his cabinet, Trudeau signalled his intention to put gender equality and the empowerment of women at the heart of his international development strategy. When asked why he placed such emphasis on gender parity, Trudeau simply replied, "Because it's 2015."

Ten days after being sworn in as Prime Minister he hit the ground running. He left for the G20 Summit in Antalya, Turkey, then went on to Manila to attend the Asia Pacific Economic Forum. There, Trudeau eclipsed President Barack Obama's star power. They cemented their relationship and traded barbs about the weight of their respective offices. "Justin, I know Canadians are incredibly inspired by your message of hope and change. I just want to point out that I had no grey hair when I took office seven years ago. So if you don't want to have grey hair like me you have to start dyeing it soon," the President said.

Traditionally, Prime Ministers live at 24 Sussex Drive, a 35-room mansion that is the Canadian equivalent of 10 Downing Street, but the century-old mansion had been neglected by at least three previous office holders and was in need of costly repair. Trudeau instead opted to live in Rideau Cottage, a 22-room Georgian Revival mansion on the sprawling grounds of the Governor General's residence.

The 42nd session of Parliament opened in December with a pledge to "restore Canadians' trust in their public institutions…(which) will include consulting on and implementing electoral reforms." He was interviewed by the *New York Times*, where he echoed his father's sentiment that "uniformity is neither desirable nor possible" in a country the size of Canada. Pierre Trudeau had been fond of quoting Henri Bourassa, a 19th century Quebec politician whose thoughts influenced his concept of Canada: "We have in our country the patriotism of Ontarians, the patriotism of Quebecers, and the patriotism of Westerners, but there is no Canadian patriotism." Elaborating on the theme Justin argued that, "There is no core identity, no mainstream in Canada. There are shared values – openness, respect, compassion, willingness to work hard, to be there for each other, to search for equality and justice. Those qualities are what make us the first post-national state."

As with all new and inexperienced administrations, there were embarrassments in its first few months. Trudeau's hard-drinking friend Seamus O'Regan, who had been elected in Newfoundland, took a voluntary leave of absence to deal with his alcohol abuse. O'Regan returned to Parliament a recovering alcoholic.

Hunter Too Too was removed as Minister of Fisheries and left the party within six months of his appointment after having a "consensual but inappropriate" relationship with a member of his staff and her mother. Too Too apologized, saying his judgement had been clouded because he had allowed "alcohol [to] take over [his] life." Drummed out of the party, he continues to sit in Parliament as an independent.

A minor controversy also erupted when Sophie Trudeau asked to have a second assistant and an official office of her own to help handle the overwhelming demands on her social life. It was an entirely reasonable request but mean-spirited critics griped that, because the Prime Minister's wife has no official duties, her husband should pay for whatever extra help she needed.

The US presidential election was underway when Barack Obama, at the end of his two terms in office, welcomed the Trudeaus to the White House in March 2016. It was the first state dinner to be given to a Canadian Prime Minister in 20 years. The last Prime Minister to be so honoured had been Jean Chretien in 1997 when Bill Clinton had been president. It was a memorable occasion in which guests dined on duck poutine, Alaskan halibut and roast apricot galette. Newspapers world-wide used the word "bromance" to describe the relationship between Trudeau and Obama, but the two leaders had more on their mind than diplomatic niceties. Donald Trump, a vulgar, erratic and inexperienced rabble-rouser, had just swept seven of eleven states in the United States Super Tuesday primaries and appeared to be well on his way to cap-turing the Republican presidential nomination. The *Washington Post* was the first to seize on Trudeau as "the Anti-Trump". He was asked whether someone so closely aligned to Obama's way of thinking could ever work with a Trump administration. Trudeau diplomatically sidestepped the issue. "I think we're going to see what Americans are made of in this upcoming election," he smiled, then added that he was prepared to work with the next president, no matter who it might be. In March 2016 it seemed improbable that a Trump presidency was possible.

During a visit in April to the Perimeter Institute for Theoretical Physics, Trudeau uncharacteristically pretended to be something he isn't when he gave the impression that he was on top of the field of quantum physics. He baited a reporter into asking him about the subject and then, apparently off the top of his head, launched into a sound bite to show just how knowledgeable he is. "A regular computer bit is either a one or a zero, either off or on," he explained. "A quantum state can be much more complex than that because, as we know, things can be both particle and wave at the same time, and the uncertainty around quantum states allows us to encode more information into a much smaller computer. So that's what is exciting about quantum computing."

It didn't take a rocket scientist to know that he had been briefed beforehand and that the pat answer had been rehearsed. It was a clever tactic. He used the explanation to distract reporters who wanted to talk about more substantial issues.

While Trudeau enjoys the international attention, he is less enthused about the routine requirements of his appearance in Parliament. He skipped half of the daily sessions, and his petulant, short-tempered behaviour was on full display on May 18, 2016, when the House was about to vote on Bill C-14, legislation that would allow doctor-assisted suicide. Goaded by a clutch of NDP MPs, who delayed the vote by blocking

Conservative whip Gordon Brown from taking his seat, Trudeau marched across the aisle and elbowed a female MP as he physically escorted Brown to his seat, later bellowing "Get the fuck out of the way." It was a distressing altercation but the NDP milked it for all it was worth. Trudeau was forced to admit that his behaviour was "not appropriate and shouldn't have happened." In an apology to the Speaker he added, "No amount of escalation or mood in this House justifies my behaviour. I made a mistake. I regret it. I am looking to make amends."

In July, he marched in Toronto's Gay Pride parade and attended a church service in the Metropolitan Community Church where he declared "It shouldn't be a big thing that a Prime Minister walks in a Pride parade, and from now on it won't be."

Trudeau set out for Beijing in August "to reset Canada's relationship with China." He was not an innocent in China as his father had claimed to be in 1960 when he toured the country with Jacques Hébert. Pierre had first gone to China in 1948 and it was Pierre Trudeau, not Richard Nixon, who was the first Western leader to open diplomatic relations with Beijing in 1970.

Justin and his brother Alexandre had been fascinated by China from childhood as well as by their father's travels. He took them as teenagers on a private visit in 1990, a year after the Tiananmen crackdown. In what seemed to be an off-hand remark in 2013, Justin expressed a level of admiration for China: "Their basic dictatorship is actually allowing them to turn their economy around on a dime." He wasn't speaking to a Canadian audience when he said that. He was already sending signals to the Chinese that when he became Prime Minister he would be willing to forge the kind of Third Option his father had tried to negotiate with Beijing in the 1970s in order to get out from under the economic and cultural domination of the United States.

Weeks before Trudeau's trip, his national security advisor and point man, Daniel Jean, met with Chinese authorities and agreed to establish a "positive, robust relationship" with the Chinese by negotiating trading agreements and exploring an extradition treaty. Trudeau presented the Chinese President Xi Jinping and Premier Li Keqiang with medallions bearing the image of Canadian doctor Norman Bethune, a hero in China, part of a limited edition set struck in 1973 when Pierre Trudeau visited Mao Zedong. The Chinese were not immune to Justin's charm offensive. *The Chongquing Morning Post* was smitten: "He has a beautiful face and is known as the best looking Prime Minister in Canadian history." Harper's government got pandas; Trudeau was rewarded with the release of Kevin Garratt, a Pentecostal minister whom the Chinese had held for two years as a spy. Trudeau dismissed concerns from human rights activists that a treaty with the Chinese would endorse systematic abuses and violate Canada's Charter of Rights and Freedoms on the grounds that there are no reliable safeguards. Garratt's release came the same week that Trudeau's brother Alexandre had his book about his travels in China, *Barbarian Lost,* published and less than a week before Chinese premier Li

Keqiang arrived in Ottawa for an official visit. (Early in 2017, Trudeau dispatched John McCallum, who had been his Minister of National Defence and Immigration, to Beijing as Canada's ambassador. In March of 2017 the government approved a Chinese takeover of a Montreal high-tech firm that produced ITF fibre laser technologies, which national security agencies had previously warned would pose a threat to Western military technology.)

When Trudeau came back from the Orient he took to the stage with billionaire philanthropist Bill Gates and U2 front man Bono at an international conference on infectious diseases in Montreal, then flew to New York for his debut at the United Nations. In a remarkably succinct speech, he described Canada as a "modest country," one that was not perfect but that got one important thing right by opening its doors to the world's refugees:

> In Canada, we see diversity as a source of strength, not weakness. Our country is strong not in spite of our differences, but because of them. And make no mistake: we have had many failures, from the internment of Ukrainian, Japanese and Italian Canadians during the World Wars; to our turning away boats of Jewish and Punjabi refugees; to the shamefully continuing marginalization of Indigenous Peoples. What matters is that we learn from our mistakes, and recommit ourselves to doing better. To that end, in recent months, Canadians have opened their arms and their hearts

to families fleeing the ongoing conflict in Syria. And from the moment they arrived, those 31,000 refugees were welcomed – not as burdens, but as neighbours and friends. As new Canadians. That effort brought Canadians together. In an almost unprecedented fashion, the government worked with the business community, engaged citizens and civil society to help the newcomers adapt to their new country. We are going to refuse to give in to the pressure of trading our cherished values for easy votes. The world expects better from us, and we expect better from ourselves. In the end, my friends, there is a choice to be made. Strong, diverse, resilient countries like Canada didn't happen by accident, and they won't continue without effort. Every single day, we need to choose hope over fear, and diversity over division. Fear has never fed a family nor created a single job. And those who exploit it will never solve the problems that have created such anxiety.

CHAPTER FOURTEEN

Donald Trump was elected the 45th President of the United States on November 8, 2016, the same day that Trudeau announced that he was leaving for Cuba, Argentina, and then Peru, where he was going to participate in the Asia Pacific Economic Conference. Although the reckless and chaotic Trump campaign had mesmerized the world, few actually expected him to win. Trudeau took the results in his stride: "We are going to keep working with people right around the world. We're going to work with our neighbours, and I am going to work with president-elect Trump's administration as we move forward in a positive way, not just for Canadians, but for the whole world."

Trudeau had hoped to meet with Fidel Castro in Havana. The Trudeau family had had a warm rapport with the Cuban leader ever since Castro first met Pierre in 1976. The two leaders had developed a genuine friendship that continued until Trudeau's death. But Castro was gravely ill and unable to meet Justin. Instead, Castro's brother treated him to an informal dinner at Restaurante Café del Oriente in the heart of old Havana, where Trudeau reassured the Cubans that Trump's victory would have no bearing on the "true friendship" between Havana and Ottawa. Diplomatic relations between the two countries had been established in 1945 and Canada never followed Washington's lead in breaking relations with

Cuba following the 1959 revolution that brought Fidel Castro to power. In fact, Canada had been critical of the US trade embargo with Cuba and, in the summer of 2015, the Harper government had been instrumental in helping the Obama administration restore diplomatic relations with Havana after 55 years by providing a venue for the negotiations. When Castro died two weeks later, Trudeau was in Liberia. He spoke as his father's son when he offered his condolences on "behalf of all Canadians," who joined the people of Cuba in mourning the loss of this "remarkable leader." His sympathetic remarks drew a lot of heat, especially from Trump supporters in the United States and Conservatives at home who chided him for his "slobbering adulation" of the Communist revolutionary leader. During his first year in office Trudeau had met a dozen world leaders, including US President Barack Obama, Chinese President Xi Jinping, German Chancellor Angela Merkel, British Prime Minister David Cameron, and he had had a brief encounter with Russian President Vladimir Putin. "International relationships often come down to personal relationships. I've seen it from my father, but to engage in formal and more casual conversations with leaders from around the world has truly reminded me of how important it is that we establish strong connections so that we can, yes, work together on issues where we align, and agree to disagree."

One year after his election, Trudeau's personal popularity continued to soar. His approval rating stood at 68 per cent even though his government's domestic track record was turning out to be spotty. According to one calculation, Trudeau had made 219 promises during the election campaign, but only 34 had been kept and 26 had been broken. The long-term census had been restored, a child benefit program had been implemented, his goal to bring in 25,000 Syrian refugees had been met and there were provisions for increased infrastructure spending. In an interview with the CBC's Anna Maria Tremonti, marking the first anniversary of his election, Trudeau acknowledged that "there is an awful lot more to do," but he defended his "sunny ways" approach to government. "We spend a lot of time travelling across the country listening to people, talking about their hopes and dreams and listening to their concerns…" He also told Tremonti that the biggest challenge he faced was "getting the balance right between economy and environment," and getting energy resources to market in sustainable ways. "Creating economic growth and protecting the important balance that previous governments certainly didn't get right – that we are very much focused on getting."

In November 2016, Trudeau was in Britain where, "in the best interests of Canada," he gave the final approval to a controversial $7 billion expansion to the Texas-based Kinder-Morgan Trans Canada Pipeline. The expansion would triple the capacity of the existing line which moved oil from Alberta across the mountains through Jasper National Park to oil shipping terminals in Burnaby, BC. He also approved another $7 billion project that would replace the existing Enbridge 3 international pipeline between Alberta and Wisconsin with bigger pipes. "It is a major win for Canadian workers, Canadian families and the Canadian economy." While Trudeau agreed to expand lines that were already built, he rejected another proposal from Enbridge to build an $8 billion twin pipeline from Bruderheim, Alberta, to Kitimat, BC.

At the same time, Trudeau insisted that Canada was still "a climate leader" and he pledged to follow Alberta's lead to introduce a carbon tax, phase out coal-powered plants, cap greenhouse gas emissions from the oil patch, and develop alternative sources of energy. Expansion of the Kinder-Morgan line was especially problematic. Two thirds of the First Nations along the route had no objections to the plan. But some tribes were concerned about the damage to the environment in the event of a spill and about the increased tanker traffic along the Pacific coast, and they launched a firestorm of protest. In all fairness, more Canadians understand and approve of his position than don't. As Trudeau would remind an energy industry conference in Texas, Canada is the world's fifth largest producer of oil: "No country would find 173 billion barrels of oil in the ground and just leave them there. The resource will be developed. Our job is to ensure that this is done responsibly, safely and sustainably. Nothing is more essential to the US economy than access to a secure, reliable source of energy. Canada has that source."

The apparent contradiction between someone "who cares about the environment" and his announcement seemed to be a betrayal of his promise to consult with those communities affected before a decision was made final. But as Trudeau has said, leadership sometimes requires taking a stand that not everyone admires or agrees with. "Leadership comes from moments where you stand up and say something difficult or controversial and it pushes back against people who might otherwise support you. It demonstrates your capacity to stand for what you believe in, not just what is popular. That is what all of us are looking for – someone who is going to stand up for what they believe in."

The announcement put an end to his honeymoon with many of his Green supporters. His approval rating slipped somewhat, especially in British Columbia, where the Liberals have 17 seats, some of them in the area of the expansion. "He presents himself as an ally with our ink on his body," griped one Haida resident, Delvina Lawrence, referring to Trudeau's Raven tattoo when talking to *Macleans*, "but we feel he has stabbed us in the back." A follow-up assessment written by environmentalist Bill McKibben, which appeared in *The Guardian*, branded Trudeau as a "stunning hypocrite" and suggested his position on oil pipelines and global warming was "a disaster.":

> Justin Trudeau sure is cute, the planet's only sovereign leader who appears to have recently quit a boy band. And he's mastered so beautifully the politics of inclusion: compassionate to immigrants, insistent on including women at every level of government. Give him great credit where it's deserved: in lots of ways he's the anti-Trump, and it's no wonder

Canadians swooned when he took over. But when it comes to the defining issue of our day, climate change, he's a brother to the old orange guy in DC. Not rhetorically: Trudeau says all the right things, over and over. But those words are meaningless if you keep digging up more carbon and selling it to people to burn, and that's exactly what Trudeau is doing. He's hard at work pushing for new pipelines through Canada and the US to carry yet more oil out of Alberta's tar sands, which is one of the greatest climate disasters on the planet.

After a year of wrangling, eleven of Canada's 13 provincial and territorial premiers met in Vancouver in December where they signed a Pan Canadian framework to reduce greenhouse gas emissions by agreeing to implement a carbon price tax. The two hold-outs, Saskatchewan Premier Brad Wall and Manitoba's Brian Pallister, both Conservatives, insist the tax is unconstitutional, and Wall has threatened legal action, claiming such a tax would harm the petroleum industry without doing anything to reduce greenhouse gas emissions.

The Vice President of the United States, Joe Biden, nearing the end of his term in office, arrived in Ottawa for a farewell state dinner in December. Trudeau had had every reason to believe that the Democrats would win the US election and that he would be dealing with Hillary Clinton as president. Trudeau's team had irritated Clinton in 2014 while he was still learning the ropes as party leader even before she declared she was running for the Democratic nomination. The Liberals had tried to cash in on her appearance at an apolitical event in Ottawa by aggressively pushing for a photo opportunity. Without her knowledge, the party had been promoting a contest that encouraged people to make a modest donation to win the chance to win a flight to Ottawa and a ticket to hear Clinton speak. Hillary may have been annoyed with Trudeau at the time, but it was an inconsequential incident. Most Canadians would have preferred to deal with a Clinton administration. Biden's visit had been arranged well before the US election presumably in anticipation of the transition from Obama to a Clinton presidency. At the dinner in Biden's honour, the vice president didn't mention Donald Trump by name, but stated that genuine world leaders were in short supply and appealed to Trudeau to "shepherd the world through a period of uncertainty."

As a result of the stunning upset in the United States, Trudeau would have to build a political relationship with Trump from scratch. Whatever his personal preference, he remained neutral during the campaign, and understood that relations between the two countries were bigger than any one president. "We share a purpose, our two countries, where we want to build places where the middle class and those working hard to join it have a chance," he told a a group of young people the day after the election and he pledged to work with a Trump administration "not just for Canadians and Americans but for the whole world."

CHAPTER FIFTEEN

December 31, 2016 was a big night in Ottawa. The 150th anniversary of Canadian confederation was ushered in on New Year's Eve with the Fire of Friendship torch rally and a spectacular fireworks display on Parliament Hill. More than 400 youngsters each holding a torch formed a glowing chain in an impressive ceremony as the centennial flame was lit anew. But Trudeau was nowhere to be found. He appeared in a videotaped message to say the evening represented a "once in a lifetime opportunity to ring in the New Year together." But he wasn't there in person and no one from his office would say where the Prime Minister was. In fact he had left the country for Bell Island in the Bahamas for a secret meeting with the outgoing US Secretary of State, John Kerry seeking Kerry's advice on how best to deal with Donald Trump and to discuss with him the implications of the incoming administration's effect on geopolitics.

Accompanying the Prime Minister on the trip were Liberal Party President Anna Gainey, MP Seamus O'Regan and their spouses.

Bell Island is a private domain owned by the Aga Kahn, one of the world's richest men. Trudeau disingenuously suggested he had been on a family vacation. But when it turned out that he had used a private helicopter to get to the island and that taxpayers had been billed $250,000 for the trip, Andrew Scheer, then a contender for the leadership of the Conservative party filed a complaint with the Ethics Commissioner, Mary Dawson. Dawson eventually ruled that by accepting the invitation Trudeau had indeed violated conflict of interest rules.

The Aga Kahn had been a friend of the Trudeau family since 1972 when Pierre Trudeau abandoned standard immigration protocol to allow 6,000 Ugandan refugees of South Asian descent who were threatened by dictator Idi Amin to seek asylum in Canada. (His half sister, Princess Yasmin Aga Kahn, the daughter of actress Rita Hayworth, befriended Trudeau's mother, Margaret, in the 70s.) The Kahn is the Imam of the Zazari Ismalis and was made an honorary Canadian citizen by the Harper government for his philanthropy. His charitable foundation has built a museum of Islamic art and Muslim culture in Toronto, the Global Centre for Pluralism in Ottawa and a park in Edmonton.

In her ruling, the Ethics Commissioner concluded that the Aga Khan may have been Pierre Trudeau's friend, but not Justin's. Justin, she discovered, had had no direct dealings with the Aga Kahn for at least 30 years and concluded the invitation for Trudeau and Kerry to meet on his island would not have been extended "had there not been official interactions between the government of Canada and the Aga Khan and had Mr Trudeau not become a significant player on the Canadian political scene." Trudeau later apologised for what he called a lapse in judgement and promised to check with the Ethics Commissioner before accepting such invitations in the future.

The uproar over Trudeau's trip to the Bahamas at taxpayer's expense caused him to skip a trip to Davos and confront Canadians and answer questions from the public in a carefully staged town hall format, an exercise in public relations that allowed his critics to blow off steam and question him. Trudeau listens with an ear to adjusting his policies, evaluating the measure of public acceptance for change. It was a largely effective trip except for one incident in Sherbrooke, Quebec where Trudeau once again tripped over language politics. In a streak of petulance he responded in French to several questions asked in English about mental health care in the region. "Thank you for using one of our country's two official languages, but since we are in Quebec I'll respond in French," he replied, setting off another storm of controversy. What he implied was that official bilingualism in Canada meant that only French be spoken in Quebec and English be used everywhere else in the country. His reasoning was especially perplexing in Quebec's Eastern Townships, an area of the country which was originally settled by United Empire Loyalists where people are civil, bilingual, and generally attempt to reply to each other in the language in which they are addressed. Trudeau tried to dodge the uproar by stating that while he supports official bilingualism he "understands the importance of speaking French and defending the French language in Quebec."

The explanation was too clever by half. Whatever the motivation, it was a foolish time and place to play linguistic politics. Under Treasury Board guidelines, Sherbrooke is listed as a bilingual service area, where Canadians who deal with the federal government have the right to be served in either English or French. Trudeau's gaffe was not lost on the leader of the

Quebec separatist party, Jean-François Lisée, who tweeted that Trudeau "was out of his depth on matters of language."

While Trudeau was touring the country Donald Trump was inaugurated as the President of the United States. James Comey, whom Trump would later fire as director of the Federal Bureau of Investigation voiced the opinion that the new president was "outside the realm of normal," and perhaps even "crazy". Justin's father, Pierre, once described Canada's relationship with the United States as that of sleeping with an elephant. "No matter how friendly or even-tempered the beast, one is affected by every twitch and grunt." But Trump was no mere elephant. One Liberal strategist referred to him as "a monkey with a machine gun." Within his first two weeks in office Trump signed an executive order signalling a national security plan that blanketed all immigrants from the Muslim world as suspected terrorists. No sooner had Trump issued his executive order, than Trudeau tweeted a message of support to Muslims seeking sanctuary in Canada.

In order to deal with the unpredictable president and his administration, a special department within the Prime Minister's Office was created. Headed by Brian Clow, a former advisor to Ontario Premier Kathleen Wynn, the office has been designed to monitor US-Canada relations and offer a measured response to the President's wildly erratic dealings with foreign governments. Before his meeting with Trump Trudeau shuffled his cabinet, moving Stéphane Dion from the front lines as Minister of Foreign Affairs replacing him with Chrystia Freeland, who was proving to be a thoughtful, sane and cool minister. He named his immigration minister, John

McCallum, who had been Defence Minister in Jean Chretien's cabinet, as Ambassador to China. McCallum was replaced by Ahmed Hussen, a Muslim who fled Somalia for Canada in 1993 when he was 16 and became a Toronto lawyer. The question as to whether Hussen might be persona non grata in the United States was raised when Trump banned travel to the US from seven Muslim countries, including Somalia. If Hussen was at all concerned, he didn't show it. "Yes, I was born in Somalia, but I took my oath of citizenship to (Canada) 15 years ago," he replied. "I am Canadian."

With his cabinet shuffle Trudeau demonstrated that he was prepared to play the political game if needed. He got rid of his old rival Stéphane Dion, whom he could barely tolerate, and at the same time sent a clear signal to Washington that he would not be intimidated by Trump. Trudeau then recruited former Progressive-Conservative Prime Minister Brian Mulroney and Mulroney's former chief of staff and Canada's former Ambassador to Washington, Derek Burney, as informal envoys to lobby the Republicans in Congress. Mulroney had negotiated both the Canadian-United States Free Trade Agreement and the North American Free Trade Agreement, which eliminated barriers to trade in goods and services between the two countries. Admittedly, there were irritants on both sides. The average US tariff for all imported goods is 3.4 per cent. Canada's average was 15 per cent, including a 218 per cent tariff on imported dairy products.

Retired Lt.-General Andrew Leslie was also brought in to lobby his contacts in the US military. Described by the *New York Times* as "the doughnut strategy," it demonstrated that Trudeau could rise above partisan politics without being a Trump sycophant. In dealing with Trump the Canadian policy is basically to humour him in person. But when serious policy and Canadian interests are concerned, to ignore him, and instead cultivate people in the oval office, state governors, business leaders and state senators. "The idea is to deal with Trump as you would deal with anyone who suffers from impaired judgement," explains a source within the PMO. "You acknowledge the problem, take Trump's tweets with a grain of salt, tread carefully and work your way around him."

Anyone who can make a contribution to "the movement" is welcome in Trudeau's tent. Among Justin's strengths is that he "knows what he doesn't know," observes one deputy minister, and in most instances he trusts his civil servants to come up with what they do best.

On January 29, 2017, a gunman, inspired in part by his admiration for Trump's racist rhetoric, walked into a mosque in Quebec City and murdered eight Muslims at prayer. It was a trying time as Trudeau attended funerals for the victims in both Montreal and Quebec City. "As a country, we will rise from this darkness stronger and more unified than ever before – that is who we are," he told mourners.

CHAPTER SIXTEEN

Turbulence was in the air as Justin Trudeau flew to Washington with five cabinet ministers in tow on February 13 for his first meeting with President Trump. Traditionally a newly inaugurated president pays his first foreign visit to Canada. But wary of protest demonstrations in Ottawa the increasingly bellicose president preferred to remain in Washington. When, in fact, Trump did make his first visit to a foreign country, it was to Saudi Arabia, not Canada.

Trudeau's flight to the American capital was delayed on the tarmac by a heavy snowfall. By the time the high level Canadian delegation landed in Washington the amateurs in the White House were trying to contain the political storm about to break that day: Trump's security advisor, Lt.-Gen Michael Flynn was about to be fired after only three weeks on the job when it was learned that Flynn's telephone conversations with Russian officials had compromised his position.

The chaos in the West Wing wasn't evident as Trudeau arrived and the stage-managed script for the four hour visit unfolded without incident. The Canadians had laid the groundwork by enlisting the President's daughter Ivanka to help launch an endeavour known as the United States-Canada Council for the Advancement of Women Entrepreneurs, a task force designed "to help women stay in the workforce and address barriers facing female entrepreneurs." Trudeau also appealed to Trump's vanity and gave the president a photograph of Trump with Prime Minister Pierre Trudeau that had been taken in 1981 at the Waldorf Astoria in New York. After the meeting Trudeau easily took control of the requisite joint press conference, fielding questions in French and in English. Asked about Trump's toxic immigration policies and the Syrian refugee crisis, Trudeau acquitted himself with a passive aggressive response. "The last thing Canadians expect is for me to come down and lecture another country on how they should choose to govern themselves. My role is to govern in such a way that reflects the Canadian approach and its positive example to the world." Trudeau walked away from the meeting with reassurances that, for the moment, Trump would not rip up the North American Free Trade Agreement as he had threatened during the campaign, but agreed that it might be "tweaked" in the best interests of both countries to improve the agreement. Trump was wary of Trudeau, and White House officials say the President didn't trust him because of his friendship with the Obamas. Trump thought Trudeau a "pushover." Within months of their first meeting, Trump denounced the trade agreement as "a disaster" and accused Canada of using the accord to take advantage of American workers and farmers. Trump vowed to move "very very quickly," to renegotiate the agreement, and in April threatened to impose duties as high as 25 per cent against Canada's softwood lumber exports. No sooner had Trudeau left Washington, Trump announced he was going to rip up the deal altogether and start from scratch. Alarmed by the president's impulsive behaviour, Trump's son in law and senior advisor, Jared Kushner took the unusual step of intervening and opened the lines of communication by arranging a telephone call between Trudeau and Trump. During the call Trudeau reminded the president that Canada is the most important foreign market for 35 states, almost all of them states that had voted for Trump.

He advised Trump that scrapping the deal wasn't that easy and would harm American interests and the very people Trump had promised to help during his campaign. "You cannot thicken this border without hurting the middle class on both sides of it," Trudeau told Trump. "Any two countries are going to have issues that will be irritants to their relationship. Having a good constructive working relationship allows us to work through those irritants." The then Mexican president Enrique Peña Nieto weighed in with a call of his own to the White House. Two days later Trump reversed himself. He told reporters that he had changed his mind because he liked "both of the gentlemen (who called) very much. The president of Mexico, who I have a very good relationship called me, and also the Prime Minister of Canada, who I have a very good relationship. They called me. They said 'rather than terminate NAFTA could you please renegotiate.' I respect their countries very much. The relationship is very special, and I said 'I will hold on the termination. Let's see if we can make it a fair deal. But we have to make a fair deal that is good for the United States.' They understand that."

On May 18 the White House advised Congress that the administration wanted NAFTA to be "modernized," and gave Congress a 90-day period to determine just what in the agreement Trump wanted to re-negotiate.

Trudeau has consistently responded to Trump's rants by calling for "a thoughtful, fact-based conversation on how to move forward in a way that protects both our consumers and our agricultural producers." Asked by John Micklethwait, the editor in chief of *Bloomberg News*, for an opinion of Trump, Trudeau was ever the diplomat. "I've learned that he listens. He is a little bit unlike many politicians. That might be enough. Leave that sentence right there," Trudeau replied. "As politicians we are trained to say something and stick with it, whereas he has shown that if he says one thing, then actually hears good counterarguments or good reason why he should shift his position, he will take a different position, if it's a better one, if the arguments win him over. There is a challenge in that for electors. But there is also an opportunity for people who engage with him to try and work to achieve a beneficial outcome." In August the United States launched the lengthy process to re-negotiate the deal.

Trump's election has increasingly thrust Trudeau into a spotlight in a role he neither expected nor welcomed as a bulwark against the rising tide of isolationism. "Now Canada is the outspoken defender of values that Americans have long embraced as their own," wrote the *Washington Post's* Ishaan Tharoor. "For thousands of Americans now marching against Trump, Trudeau represents much that they are missing in their current president, from his celebration of feminism and his belief in man-made climate change, to his openness to other cultures and his willingness to apologize for his nation's past misdeeds." Similarly, the German newspaper *Die Welt* referred to Trudeau as "The Anti-Trump," and as a voice of reason in a world in which countries were becoming increasingly isolationist. The United Kingdom was preparing to leave the European Union, turmoil in Syria and in the Middle East continued to fester, the US relationship with Russia was increasingly unpredictable and the French presidential election exposed new social fissures and fault lines. In Germany for talks with Angela Merkel, Trudeau lent his support to the Canada-European Union Comprehensive Economic and Trade Agreement (CETA) at a black tie dinner in Hamburg. The deal will eliminate 98 per cent of the tariffs between Canada and the European Union, making many European imports to Canada cheaper than European imports to the United States. However, Trudeau warned the corporate leaders in the room who stand to profit from the arrangement that they could no longer ignore "the concerns of our workers and our citizens. We have to address the root cause of their worries and get real about the changing economy that is impacting people's lives." Perhaps in anticipation of his own government's budget plans, Trudeau told the St. Matthew's Day banquet that "Citizens across the political spectrum are looking for a voice, and so far they are feeling a little let down." The anxiety of the working class, he added, is turning into anger, and politicians and business leaders have to think beyond their short-term responsibility to shareholders."It's time to pay a living wage, to pay your taxes, and to give your workers the benefits and peace of mind that comes with stable, full time contracts. You have an equally important long-term responsibility to your employees, their families and the communities that support you. Whether you are a business or a government, it is time to realize the anger and the anxiety we see washing over the world is coming from a real place and it is not going away."

During a meeting with the President of the European Parliament, Antonio Tahjani, Trudeau even managed to say nice things about President Trump's intentions, to help the middle class. "What I saw from the American President was a focus on getting things done for the people who supported him and who believe in him while demonstrating that good relations with one's neighbours is a great way to get things done." When Trump bombed a Syrian air base Trudeau voiced his support for the missile attack as "limited and focused action" against Bashar al-Assad. In some respects, Trudeau's and Trump's interests are similar. As Stephen Mache suggested in *Bloomburg Businessweek,* "opponents who try to paint Trudeau as shallow and stupid, miss the point: He understands the division of labour. He is the face, so that the faceless bureaucrats can do their job. His task as Prime Minister is to create the conditions under which what he considers the best policies, crafted by experts, can be implemented. He possesses an odd combination of total narcissism and complete lack of ego. If I were his political opponents, I'd fear him deeply. He can get things done with the Canadian people barely noticing, whether they like it or not."

Trudeau is a modern metrosexual who continues to attract media attention and appreciative glances wherever he goes, be it Broadway (where he and Ivanka Trump attended the Canadian smash hit *Come From Away,* about people in Newfoundland opening their homes to passengers stranded on the island after the 9-11 attacks) or a cabinet meeting in Calgary. "He enjoys leading the orchestra," says Terry DiMonte,

"He knows what he wants, he knows what he thinks is right, what he believes in, and he is not afraid to say to a room full of people, 'you've all been very helpful, but I have decided this is what we are going to do.'"

He can be unusually selfless. When 16 young men with the Humbolt Broncos hockey team were killed in an horrific highway accident in Saskatchewan in the spring of 2018, Trudeau slipped into the memorial service with one of his sons almost unnoticed and mourned with the community. However, while Trudeau seems to be open and accessible there is a line with him that no one dares cross. Trudeau has demonstrated that as Prime Minister he is very much his own man.

"For decades he has been told what he should and shouldn't do, been reminded of who his father was, and who is mother is and isn't, and at some point he tuned out and decided to do his own thing," says Marc Miller.

CHAPTER SEVENTEEN

All Prime Ministers do silly things but Canadians are still trying to make sense of Trudeau's attempt to "do his own thing," during his week long passage through India in February 2018. He arrived in New Dehli with six cabinet ministers on what his office incorrectly called "a state visit".

On a visit to Ahmedabad and to the Swaminarayan Akshardham temple in Gandhinagar, the entire family was outfitted in traditional Indian garb; Sophie wore a sari and mang tika and the children wore a churidar kurta. Then at a film industry reception Trudeau managed to upstage Bollywood stars, Shah Rukh Khan and Amir Khan, who arrived for the event in business suits. Trudeau showed up in a dazzling gold Sherwani. On a visit to a holy temple Trudeau's head was appropriately wrapped in a saffron patkah, which is worn instead of a turban as a mark of respect by those who aren't Sikhs. After three days, the costume parade began to irritate some observers as being "too Indian even for an Indian." Omar Abdullah, the former chief minister in Kashmir chided "the choreographed cuteness," as being a bit over the top. "Even we Indians don't dress this way everyday, not even in Bollywood," he tweeted. It is not clear who was responsible for the costume parade, but the finger points in the direction of Trudeau's wife, Sophie, who once said her role is to "scatter what I can of beauty in the places that I think need it, to get rid of boredom and meanness in the world," and engaged the celebrated Indian designer, Anita Dongre, to outfit the family. Dongre has designed ensembles with signature Gotta Patti embroidery for the Duchess of Cambridge and for Belgium's Queen Mathilde. Trudeau explained the trip was for the benefit of the children, "to show them the extraordinary diversity and pluralism of India."

Trudeau tried to make light of the whole affair at the annual Parliamentary Press Gallery dinner. "In spite of the wall to wall international ridicule, it was a very good trip," he quipped. He chided the press for not reporting what he achieved on the occasions that he was wearing a shirt and promised tie, and "never travel again."

But it wasn't the costume parade that was the major problem. It was the Canadian government's invitation to a convicted Sikh terrorist, Jaspal Singh Atwal to attend a couple of receptions in Mumbai, that derailed Trudeau's visit. Trudeau once boasted that he has more Sikhs in his cabinet than Indian Prime Minister Modi. Atwal's invitation (which was later rescinded) was seen in India as tacit support for the Khalistan separatist movement. When Atwal emigrated to Canada in the 1970s he was a member of the International Sikh Youth Federation. He became a Canadian citizen in 1977, then in 1984 Atwal was charged with an attack on Ujjal Dosanjh, who would later become Premier of British Columbia. The assault charges were dismissed, but one year later, Atwal was convicted of attempting to assassinate an Indian cabinet minister, Malkiat Singh Sidhu who had come to Vancouver Island on a private visit to attend a wedding. Sidhu's car was ambushed by Sikh terrorists and although he was hit by two bullets, he survived the attack. Atwal was sentenced to 20 years in prison for his role in the assassination attempt but served only five years. He became a car salesman, active as a fund raiser for the Liberals in the Fleetwood-Port Kells riding association. He was well enough known within the party to be photographed with Trudeau in 2015 and with Trudeau's wife in India.

"Trudeau's India trip from the outset was playing to a diaspora gallery back home, one in which he has been studiously ambiguous on the Khalistani ties of some of his Liberal Party's Sikh Canadian supporters," Carleton University professor Vivek Dehejia, told *The Washington Post*. "For those who are lukewarm on Trudeau, his behaviour reconfirms their impression that the rock star image hides feet of clay, and that he has been undone by his own cleverness in trying to massage the diaspora vote back home. "In an interview with author and journalist John Ivison, Gerald Butts blamed Indian Prime Minister Modi and his government who "were out to screw us and were throwing tacks under our tires to help Canadian Conservatives."

What Trudeau's flamboyant behaviour did do was irritate many voters who turned their attention to the new leader of the Canadian Conservative party, . Scheer had been culled from a herd of 13 candidates to replace Stephen Harper and had not made much of an impression following his win at the leadership convention in May. Scheer emerged to win the leadership after 13 rounds of voting as the least objectionable of the Conservative contenders. A former speaker of the House of Commons Scheer is bilingual, has roots in both the East and West, and has been described as "sensibly dull."

A tall man (6'4") with a cherubic Alfred E. Neuman smile, Andrew Scheer is, at 40, eight years younger than Trudeau. What he lacks in star power he makes up for with other qualities. He inherited a party in good financial shape, and enjoys broad support in caucus. He is personable, approachable and, unlike Trudeau, has a knack for engaging people who talk to him.

Scheer's father was a deacon at St. Patrick's Basilica and a librarian at the *Ottawa Citizen*. His mother, Mary, a nurse, died in March during the leadership race. Scheer was raised in Ottawa with his two sisters, was an altar server at St. Clements Roman Catholic church, and studied at the University of Ottawa, where he met Jill Ryan, a school teacher from Regina. He moved to Saskatchewan to be with her, and took a job as a waiter. They married at Holy Rosary Cathedral in 2003 and have five children.

A devout Roman Catholic, he opposes same sex marriage and expressed "outrage and disappointment" when Henry Morgentaler, a doctor who led the abortion movement in Canada, was awarded the Order of Canada. Although he has pledged not to "re-open or revisit" same sex marriage laws, he makes it clear that he has his own personal religious beliefs, his own faith.

"I absolutely think that each member of Parliament has a different kind of faith – a different level of faith and it is up to each member to determine how much he or she wants to incorporate into their public life. But it is an important part of my life. It is important for us to have public policy discussions in an environment where a person's religion is welcomed." Scheer campaigned on his "top five priorities" – he would balance the budget within two years of being elected, eliminate the carbon tax, lower taxes, promote free speech on universities and he would deport any asylum seekers who have entered Canada illegally. He doesn't believe governments should be in the 'news business' and has threatened to axe the news and public affairs division of the state broadcaster, the Canadian Broadcasting Corporation and its French language division, Radio Canada.

Scheer cut his political teeth working for the provincial Saskatchewan Party, for Preston Manning's Reform Party and for the short-lived, right-wing Canadian Alliance before Stephen Harper hired him to work in the Opposition Leader's office. In 2004 he ran for the Conservatives in a largely rural Saskatchewan riding, Regina-Qu'Appelle.

The seat had been held by the NDP's Lorne Nystrom, a Member of Parliament for more than 30 years. Many thought Scheer was running as a sacrificial lamb. At 24, with the odds against him, he took the seat from Nystrom. Two years later, he was named Deputy Speaker and worked with Peter Milliken, who held the job of Speaker longer than anyone else in Commons history. He spent whatever spare time he had watching the British House of Commons debates on television to acquaint himself with the work. When Stephen Harper won a majority, Scheer defeated eight other candidates after six rounds of balloting for the $240,000-a-year job. He was two weeks shy of his 32nd birthday.

During his time as Speaker, Scheer started an informal study group on Parliament Hill of the St. Thomas More Society. Named for the Chancellor of England who fell out of favour with Henry VIII over the issue of divorce, it was open to all MPs and parliamentary staff. It meets several times a year for dinner to talk about, and perhaps influence, public policy. And as a former speaker, Scheer knows procedure inside out and the Liberals will have to be truly on their game. Scheer resembles Stephen Harper, with more personality.

He's an "aw shucks" kind of guy who tosses back popcorn and likes *The Simpsons*. He will have to convince Canadians that he best represents their values.

Scheer has exploited the "fear of the other" to appeal to his Conservative base, and has promised to rid the country of "illegal immigrants" and asylum seekers who have crossed the border into Canada from the United States following President Trump's election.Scheer has tried to gain traction from the government's $10.5-million payout to a Canadian child soldier, Omar Khadar, who was captured in Afghanistan when he was 15 and accused by the Americans of throwing a hand grenade which killed a US Army medic. Khadar was held and tortured in Guantanamo prison for ten years in violation of what the Canadian Supreme Court ruled were "the most basic Canadian standards of the way children should be treated." The previous Liberal government was complicit in the torture, and the Supreme Court ruling opened the doors to a $20-million civil suit filed by Khadar's lawyers which he almost certainly would have won. Rather than spend more money on litigation, the Trudeau government decided on the payout. Most Canadians were outraged. Scheer attempted with some success to portray Trudeau in the most simplistic terms as making a millionaire out of a self-confessed Al-Qaeda terrorist. Whether it will be an issue in the election campaign is yet to be determined. Trudeau apologized to Khadar and defended the government payout saying "this is not about the merits of the Khadar case. The Charter of Rights and Freedoms protects all Canadians, everyone of us, even when it is uncomfortable. When the government violates those Charter rights, we all end up paying for it."

Although the Conservatives won a by-election in Sagueney-Lake St. Jean in 2018, Scheer's leadership abilities came into question when Maxime Bernier, whom he narrowly defeated for the leadership, quit the party in August, 2018, and started his own Libertarian splinter group the People's Party of Canada.

If Canadians want to vote for an authentic Sikh, they need look no further than Jagmeet "Jimmy" Singh, the cutting edge Toronto born criminal lawyer who the NDP elected to replace Tom Mulcair in October 2017. Singh is a practicing Sikh who with his colourful turbans represents a generational change in Canadian politics. Like Trudeau, he is another vanity politician trained in the martial arts, exudes charm and has made it into the pages of GQ magazine. A former member of the Ontario legislature, he is a product of multiculturalism and his election to lead the party came a century after a boat load of Sikhs – all of them British subjects – were denied entry into Canada after a government official of the day declared Canada to be "a White Man's Country."

Not only is he fluent in French and English, but he speaks Hindi, Tamil and Punjabi. He preaches a more aggressive line than Trudeau and calls for fundamental changes to the criminal justice system, including the decriminalization of hard drugs. It remains to be seen whether the majority of Canadians are comfortable with him as the leader of a national party.

Unless Singh can persuade a million voters who deserted the New Democrats and helped elect Trudeau in 2015 to return to the fold, the party appears destined to remain the social conscience of Parliament.

CHAPTER EIGHTEEN

Donald Trump threw out the rule book on international trade relations on May 31, 2018 when, in the interests of what he insisted was "US National security," he unleashed a trade war with Canada and imposed a punitive 25 per cent tariff on steel imports and a 25 per cent import on aluminum. The action signaled one of the lowest points in the history of US-Canada relations. In what was described as a "testy" telephone exchange, Trudeau rejected the suggestion that Canada was a risk to US national security as an insulting and unacceptable affront to Canadians. He demanded that Trump explain. It is not certain whether the president was trying to defuse the tense exchange when he quipped: "Didn't you guys burn down the White House in 1812?" The following week Trump's Doctor Jekyll morphed into a full blown Mr Hyde when he arrived late for a G-7 meeting in Charlevoix, Quebec.

The president has yet to pay an official state visit to Canada, but he spent a few hours in Malbaie, Quebec, during a meeting of the G-6. Following his whirlwind visit he left without signing the declaration which affirmed the group's "shared values," of freedom, democracy, the rule of law and the respect for human rights.

The spat over tariffs and his insistence that Russia be restored to G-7 had fouled his mood. As Trump left for a meeting with North Korea's Kim Jong-un, Trudeau held a news conference in which he said he would not be "pushed around" by the United States. It was an innocuous remark which set off yet another Trump tirade. Aboard Air Force One Trump called Trudeau a "weak and dishonest" leader. The president suggested that Trudeau held a news conference because he thought he, Donald Trump, was out of earshot... "I get onto Air Force One and (Justin) doesn't understand that Air Force One has 22 televisions. So I come on – they have televisions in closets – they have televisions in areas that no place has. Unlimited budget. Air Force One. Right? So I get on the plane and I see Justin Trudeau Prime Minister of Canada saying 'Canadians will not be bullied by the United States.' I said what are we doing here? The fact is that Canada has a 275 per cent tariff on dairy products. Little thing called dairy product. Their lumber is a disaster with us, I say. Why aren't we using our own lumber?"

To add insult to injury Trump's trade advisor, Peter Navarro, suggested that there was "a special place in hell for Trudeau," who he claimed enaged in "bad faith diplomacy." As the negotiations continued, Trump called Canada "the worst country to negotiate with," and branded Chrystia Freeland as "very nasty," which, incidentally only enhanced her star quality in Canada. It was typical Trump, whose mantra is "destablization creates an American advantage."

For all of Trump's bluster, a new NAFTA was negotiated by the Canadian team who contained Trump by working with his son-in-law. The agreement, known in Canada as CUSMA (Canada, US, Mexico Agreement) isn't all that different than the old one. It was signed in November, 2018, but its ratification by the United States has been stalled in Congress.

Trudeau used Trump's election as a convenient excuse to break a campaign promise to reform the electoral system, which, if the opposition can be believed, he made at least 1,800 times. Trudeau rejected a parliamentary committee's recommendation that a system of proportional representation be put to a vote in a national referendum. In breaking the promise he said he was not prepared to implement a fragmented state of government where at least six parties might be represented in Parliament and give momentum to extremists. "It would be irresponsible to do something that harms Canada's stability, "he declared.

Meanwhile, his domestic agenda appears to be on hold. Electoral reform is dead in the water. His government has introduced omnibus bills, a practice which he promised to eliminate before he was elected. Tax hikes on the rich have been deferred. A 185-billion dollar infastructure program designed to "attract private sector invesment to projects that are in the public interest" is virtually dormant. He has backtracked on a promise to give First Nations a veto over development on their territory and respect their treaty rights. His commitment to work with indigenous people on "a nation to nation" basis has been compromised. Trudeau wavers on the point of his combat mission against ISIS. He has legalized cannibis, but each of the provinces and municipalities have implemented their own laws on how pot is distributed in their respective jurisdictions. As a result, there are now more arrests for illegal possession and distribution of pot than when it was illegal.

Eighteen by-elections since 2016 have changed little in the House of Commons. One Liberal backbencher crossed the floor to sit as Conservative in 2018. But it was a by-election won by the Green Party in the spring of 2019 that has given momentum to the once marginal party headed by environmentalist Elizabeth May. May was born in the United States but grew up in Nova Scotia where she obtained her law degree. Elected to Parliament in 2011, she was the only member of her party elected to Parliament until a second member from British Columbia was elected in a 2019 by-election. Then, in the Prince Edwad Island general election, the Greens increased their vote by 20 percent, won nine seats, and became the first province in which the party formed the official opposition. May's "Mission Possible," campaign, as she calls it, appears to be picking up steam, but whether it will make a signifcant breakthrough is debateable. But if the coalition that elected Trudeau in 2015 disintegrates, the Green's could pick up votes that might otherwise have gone to the Liberals. Elizabeth May gained some traction in September when 14 prominent New Democrats in New Brunswick critical of leader Jagmeet Singh quit the NDP and joined the Greens. In Quebec the nationalist Bloc Quebecois seems to have been revived under its new leader, a former member of the Quebec National Assembly, Yves-François Blanchet, and with about 20 per cent of the vote, could undermine Liberal strength in the province.

CHAPTER NINETEEN

Global warming and Trudeau's committment to promote a gradual shift from Canada's dependency on fossil fuels to alternative sources of energy has become the government's biggest challenge. While a majority of Canadians are concerned about greenhouse gas emissions and global warming they are not prepared to pay the price to reduce carbon emissions. Fighting climate change is an expensive proposition, and voters resent having to spend money out of their own pockets in an attempt to curb it. No one has ever voted for a tax, even if you can claim a rebate for it on your income tax.

British Columbia was the first to put a price on carbon pollution in 2008. When Trudeau was elected in 2015, he had the support of eight of the ten provinces for a national carbon pricing or a cap and trade program which encourages companies to invest in clean technology by putting a "cap" on the amount of carbon dioxide they are allowed to emit. Quebec had already introduced its own program in 2013, and Ontario implemented its own cap and trade program in 2015. Rachel Notley's NDP government was preparing to sign on to a national carbon tax program. In October he announced that Ottawa would impose its own levy of $50 a tonne if the provinces didn't adopt their own tax or implement a cap and trade program to fight pollution. Environmentalists had high hopes for Trudeau's climate change policy, but sceptics don't believe the atmosphere is warming. Even if it is, they say, it is too late to do anything about it as long as China, India, and Indonesia continue to spew greenhouse gas emissions into the atmosphere. Starting in June 2018, Ontario replaced a Trudeau ally Kathleen Wynne with a populist Doug Ford, who immediately scrapped Ontario's cap and trade program. New Brunswick voted the Liberals out, and in October, Quebec elected a right-wing government. In the spring of 2019 Jason Kenny, another right-wing demagogue replaced Rachel Notley's NDP government in Alberta. Saskatchewan and Ontario have launched court challenges against the federal government's right to impose the carbon tax. Although both have lost in the lower courts, they have filed a challenge in the Supreme Court, and both have lost. Trudeau made no friends in Alberta when he said that the oil sands (in which bitumen is extracted from the sand) must be phased out, remarks which he later said were misinterpreted.

The dramatic crash in oil prices has taken a heavy toll on the Alberta economy and on the Oil Sands, The balance between a low carbon economy and the development of fossil fuels that Trudeau promotes in his National Energy Strategy is under attack. When he arrived in office he found himself having to juggle four applications to build pipelines, none of which he was enthusiastic about.

The first was the 2,600 km Keystone XL Pipeline, which would stretch from Alberta to Illinois and Texas. President Obama vetoed it. Donald Trump approved it.

TransCanada Corp. had laid plans to build a pipeline

to ship oil from Alberta through Quebec to New Brunswick, a project known as Energy East. But when Trump approved Keystone XL, the project died.

Then there was the Northern Gateway, a pipeline that would run from Alberta, across the Great Bear Rain Forest to Kitimat, BC.

Also in the works was Kinder Morgan's plan to double the capacity of an existing pipeline which runs near Vancouver. Ottawa had approved the application, but 60 per cent of the province opposed the project. The election of a New Democratic Party Government put it on hold and provoked a trade war with Alberta, which wanted the project to go ahead. Indigenous groups staged disruptive protest demonstrations. Because of the political uncertainty, Kinder Morgan suspended its plans. In order to salvage the embattled project the Trudeau government (which has 17 seats in BC) killed the Northern Gateway project but bought the Kinder Morgan pipeline for $4.5 billion saying it was "a sound investment," in the best interests of Canada. It may also be because the pipeline is in China's best interests. Under an agreement negotiated by the previous Harper government, PetroChina, which invested heavily in the Oil Sands, is guaranteed access to Canadian oil.

Trudeau's admiration for China was tested in December 2018 when Canadian border security in Vancouver arrested Meng WanZhou, Huawei Telecom's chief financial officer and the daughter of the company's founder. She was arrested under a reciprocal agreement with the United States who want her extradited for financial fraud. Canada was caught in the middle of a dispute between the two countries, and the Canadian Ambassador to China, John McCallum was fired when he suggested that "It wold be great for Canada if the US dropped its request for the extradition of Meng Wanzhou." In retaliation, the Chinese arrested Michael Kovrig, a former diplomat who once worked at the Canadian Embassy in Bejing on suspicion of "gathering state secrets and intelligence for abroad," and Canadian business consultant Michael Spavor, accused of "stealing and providing state secrets for abroad." As the rift deepened the Chinese sought to cripple the Canadian Canola industry which exports 40 per cent of its crops to China. The Chinese banned imports of the grain claiming some shipments were "infected with pests" then suspended the licences of two of Canada's biggest grain exporters. The situation did nothing to endear Trudeau to Western Canadian farmers who don't always understand foreign policy agreements, and don't undertand why Trudeau is doing "Trump's bidding."

Then SNC Lavelin happened.

What was supposed to be what Gerald Butts described as a "simple plan for a small tidy cabinet shuffle," ran off the rails when Trudeau inexplicably decided to demote Jody Wilson-Raybould and offer her a position which she had often said she could not, as an an indigenous person, in all good conscience accept. It would have required her to administer the Indian Act, which Butts later told an inquiry that he "should have known that, and had we had more time, I probably would have realized that." He quietly denied that Wilson-Raybould's removal as Attorney General and Justice Minister had anything to do with her refusal to drop the charges against SNC Lavelin, and quite correctly pointed out that Prime Ministers have every right to select their cabinet ministers. He advised Trudeau that he should not set a precedent which would allow a cabinet minister to refuse a new position. He told Trudeau that if he allowed a minister to veto a cabinet shuffle by refusing to move he would soon not be able to manage cabinet. A report by the Ethics Commissioner in August vindicated Wilson-Raybould, and ruled the authority of the Prime Minister and his office was used "to circumvent, undermine and ultimately attempt to discredit the decision of the director of public prosecutions as well as the authority of Ms. Wilson-Raybould as the Crown's chief law officer." While Trudeau has said he takes "full responsibility" for his actions, he has refused to admiit what he did was wrong.

His government is not without its accomplishments, especially its Child Benefit program, a lower tax rade for middle income Canadians, its Senate reform and the creation of a national inquiry into Missing and Murdered Indigenous Women and Children.

Unemployment is markedly low.

Where Trudeau is vulnerable is in his unapologetic confidence, in his occasional petulance, and in his failure to keep his promises.

Although he was elected on a promise "to do things differently," he is a light-wing politician who has governed from the pragmatic centre. He has found a generally acceptable soft middle, a belief in progressive social change tempered with practical restraint. Marijuana was legalized in October, 2018, but its sale and distribution has been left up to the provinces to regulate. And the government has legalized assisted suicide, which depending on your views, can go either on its plus or minus side.

Many of his signature campaign promises have either been axed, muddied or deferred It is clear that the government can no longer continue to coast on Trudeau's generally sunny disposition or on its slick public relations, photo-ops and smart sock diplomacy.

Trudeau has proven himself to be a man of strong opinions, held unconvincingly. Or as *Macleans* columnist Paul Wells has written "an odour of plutocracy around the Trudeau clique is beginning to smell." There are signs that the country is beginning to suffer a degree of Trudeau fatigue. He is in danger of following in his father's footsteps. After Pierre Trudeau rode a wave of Trudeaumania to a landslide victory in 1968, he lost 38 seats in the 1972 election and was returned for a second term with a razor-thin minority.

Going into the 2019 election Trudeau does, however, have the power of the incumbent on his side. Only twice in the country's history have Prime Ministers been denied a second term – R.B. Bennett in 1935 and Alexander Mackenzie in 1878. In both cases, both had the misfortune to be elected just as the country was hit by a depression. The Canadian economy is growing 2.6 per cent faster than that of any other G-7 country, but the deficit remains a problem. Trudeau's first budget anticipated a larger deficit than the one the Liberals promised during the election campaign. His second budget anticipated a

$28.5 billion deficit. The Trump factor, too may be considered if, as generally expected, the United States heads into a recession. Still, at last count, Trudeau had 4.6 million followers on his Facebook page and hundreds of thousands of followers on Twitter. Though the warmth of Trudeau's "sunny ways" has cooled many voters are uncomfortable with the choices before them. Elections are rarely fought on terrain chosen by the incumbent and unexpected events during a campaign can derail the best laid plans. A Jihadist attack in Canada, like those in Birmingham, London and Paris, for example, would play into Scheer's hands.

Justin Trudeau still fits central casting's bill for the made-for-television movie role of a political idealist. For the moment, Scheer can't match it. Trudeau is a fine communicator, *bien dans sa peau*, as the French expression goes. Whether he shows up for a meeting with Ireland's former Taoiseach Enda Kenny wearing mismatched *Star Wars* socks (one in blue, depicting R2D2, the other in gold for C3Po), dances the Bhangra (which he does gracefully), hugs a unicorn puppet for a popular children's television show, or horses around with his three year old son, Hadrien (who was stuffed into a cabinet for a staged photo opportunity), he remains the darling of social media. His choice of funky socks themed to convey an unspoken message in support of one cause or another has attracted worldwide attention. "Rarely have a man's ankles said so much," Vanessa Friedman wrote in the *New York Times*. "The socks have been a source of applause on an international scale, a symbol of Mr Trudeau's ability to embrace multiculturalism and of his position as a next-Gen leader."

Image has been at the core of Trudeau's rise to power. But much of what has happened in his first mandate has been symbolic, not substantive. As Camosun College political science professor Daniel Reeve observes, "While Trudeau has ripped his own halo off his head and stomped it on the ground for all to see, that does not mean there is no chance of a second term."

For better or worse, Trudeau has branded Canada in his image. He represents the face that many Canadians identify with. At the same time he has gone out of his way to downplay expectations that Canada is "a magical place that is some sort of a unicorn." As he told a Women's World Summit in New York, "Like Americans, Canadians face economic uncertainty, people are worried about their future, about their kid's future. People are facing that perhaps for the first time the next generation won't have the kinds of opportunities that the last generation did. Canadians have just been able to pull together in a way that understands that we succeed better when we all succeed."